How to Teach Writing Without Going Crazy

By
Murray Suid
and Wanda Lincoln

Illustrated by Philip Chalk

This book is for
Stan Friedman and Claudia Marie

Publisher: Roberta Suid
Copy Editor: Carol Whitely
Design & Production: Scott McMorrow
Cover: Dana Mardaga
Illustrator: Philip Chalk

Also in this series: *How to Teach Reading Without Going Crazy*

Other Monday Morning publications by the authors
include: *Ten-Minute Editing Skill Builders, Ten-Minute
Grammar Grabbers, Ten-Minute Real-World Reading,
Storybooks Teach Writing, For the Love of Research, Write
Through the Year,* and *The Kids' How to Do (Almost)
Everything Guide.*

CONTENTS

INTRODUCTION

Teaching writing can be a joyful task. Few things are more rewarding than helping students express themselves with clarity and competence.

Unfortunately, if you find yourself burdened by hours of reading and correcting papers, while also meeting the demands of your school or district curriculum, the job can become something other than pleasant.

How to Teach Writing Without Going Crazy aims to help you discover—or rediscover—the creative, fulfilling dimension of this important work. This book offers a method that will enable you to manage the paperwork while sharpening your students' skills, and also building their motivation.

The **Teaching Principles** section shows how to lay the foundation for a successful writing program. These practical principles include:
• planning the year's program
• making sure students understand each assignment
• teaching students to evaluate their own work
• setting up a literacy-supporting environment

The **Writing Process** section offers quick, involving exercises for sharpening basic writing tasks: getting ideas, planning, researching, organizing, revising, and publishing.

Dozens of real-world formats are grouped in six classic writing categories: descriptive, dramatic, expository, narrative, persuasive, and poetic. This arrangement makes it easy to create a balanced program. Each step-by-step, reproducible lesson include a model to clarify the assignment.

Resources offers bonus materials, including a collection of answers to frequently asked questions.

All of the ideas presented here have been successfully tested by teachers in classrooms around the world. We believe that this material will prove useful in your classroom. We welcome your comments, questions, and suggestions. Happy writing.
    Murray Suid & Wanda Lincoln
    mmbooks@aol.com

CREATE A WRITING ENVIRONMENT

Writers know that a story's setting affects the action. The same is true for education. The environment that you create will have a major impact on students' progress as writers.

The environment will also have a big impact on you! For example, suppose that you **post clear and complete directions for carrying out an assignment** including the criteria that will be used to evaluate the finished product. Chances are now greater that the students will tackle the task with confidence and will produce first-rate work. It's also more likely that students will not need to continually ask you what they are supposed to be doing.

Whether you have a writing center or treat the entire room as a stage for literacy, the following elements belong in a well-organized, skill-oriented environment.

Displays and resources that support the writing process and help kids be independent, giving you more time for individuals and groups. Examples: peer editing checklists; self-evaluation criteria; "first draft" rubber stamp; format models; class books of student work to read during sustained silent reading; book binding tips and materials (clip art books, tape, hole punch, yarn, glue, stapler); tape recorder (for radio plays and other audio publishing); access to a computer with an online link for research and exchanging work with distant classes.

References, such as: almanacs, an atlas, a concise encyclopedia, dictionaries, grammar books, a phone book (with yellow pages), quotation books, a rhyming dictionary, a style manual, and a thesaurus.

Student writing folders, one for current assignments, and a portfolio of completed work.

And most important...a teacher who expects all students to succeed; who shows respect by listening; who asks for feedback; who balances creativity (word play, etc.) with discipline (editing, meeting deadlines); who understands that mistakes are learning opportunities; who fosters responsibility and independence, for example, by including choice in the program; who gives the "why" for assignments; and who writes with students—modeling skills and sharing the creative experience.

PLAN YOUR PROGRAM

Planning can make your job more manageable and fulfilling. The task begins by carefully studying the school's curriculum. Your creativity and individuality will be expressed within that structure. As for specifics, our planning focuses on three time frames: the *year*, the *week*, and the *day*.

PLANNING FOR THE YEAR
Like a drama, the school year breaks into a beginning, a middle, and an end. Each part offers unique opportunities.
Beginning of the year
• *Preview the program.* Education is a journey, not a game of keep-away. Students will get more from the trip if they know where they're going. For this reason, give an overview of the year's skills and formats. This will serve as a forecast (subject to change like a weather forecast).
• *Find out what your students know and can do.* Using your school's developmental continuum or grade level standards, assess their attitude towards writing, knowledge of the writing process, ability to edit for content and mechanics, and mastery of sample formats written in previous years.
Always build on what students know.
• *Introduce the writing process.* We give an overview of the steps used to produce most writing, and then refer to the steps throughout the year. (See pages 18-31.)
• *Launch ongoing activities to create continuity.* Some skill builders that we have found effective are: daily editing, word play to develop fluency, learning logs to practice self-evaluation, and journal writing to encourage self-expression.
• *Choose an autobiographical first assignment.* An example is the "Self-portrait" (page 40). This type of assignment, handled with sensitivity, helps students understand that your classroom is a safe place to tell about themselves.
Middle of the year
• *Conduct mid-year assessment.* Students can note progress in their writing skills. Help them set goals for continued improvement.
• *Review your program's forecast with the class.* If you need to make changes, you'll be modeling flexibility.
End of the year
• *Do a final assessment of student progress.* Invite students to give you written feedback on the program.
• *Give students a list of high-interest writing projects they might try on their own.*

PLANNING FOR THE WEEK

We use the week as the basic unit for teaching a format, such as the book review. Some formats need less time, and others will require more, especially if students need help with difficult format elements. The following sequence for teaching the narrative poem is only a rough framework:

• *Monday*: Introduce the format by identifying key elements and reading examples, such as "Casey at the Bat." Have pairs of students rewrite a stanza to practice the art of presenting dialogue and description in rhyme.
• *Tuesday*: Students choose subjects for their own story poems, then outline the stories. They may begin drafting.
• *Wednesday*: Students draft their poems. Near the end of the time, they share their works in progress in small groups.
• *Thursday*: Students complete their drafts. Give them editing criteria and have them revise their work with the help of peer editors.
• *Friday*: Students share their poems orally in small groups or with the whole class. In their notebooks, they review the week's work. Finally, the teacher forecasts the next week.

PLANNING FOR A DAY

By "day" we mean the block of time, about 45 minutes, devoted to a writing session. It's important to note that generally no two days are alike. Therefore, it is important to have a list of quality writing activities from which to choose when lesson planning. Here's a starter list:
• *A warm-up*: Like athletic stretching, this helps students turn their minds to writing while practicing one of the key processes, for example brainstorming. The warm-up often links to the key lesson of the day, for example, brainstorming a list of objects that could be used in a diagram project.
• *Skill practice*: An example would be paraphrasing text.
• *Guided edit*: If student work is due, we often guide them through a final check of content and mechanics, reinforcing their skills and also making our own jobs easier.
• *Teacher-directed lesson*: An example would be introducing a format or teaching a step in the writing, such as drafting.
• *Work on an assignment*: This could involve any of the major steps, such as researching, drafting, or editing.
• *Learning log*: An end-of-the-period activity in which students reflect on what they have been doing.

Some days will feature several activities, while others may focus on just one. Remember, you are the decision maker. Take your cues from your students and your yearly plan.

DEVELOP A BALANCED PROGRAM

A balanced writing program provides students with a wide range of interesting challenges and the quality instruction needed to help students achieve success. When creating your writing program, keep in mind these issues:

• **Form:** One clear responsibility of a writing teacher is to provide opportunities for students to experiment with all the major types of writing: descriptive, dramatic, expository, narrative (story), persuasive, and poetic. How many assignments should come from each group? There is no magic writing "diet." The balance you create will depend on students' past writing experiences, their skill needs, and even on your favorite formats. We do know, however, that teaching formats from each group— and the skills that go with them—will provide a firm foundation, as well as balance.

• **Audience:** Successful writers need to know how to present their ideas to all sorts of readers. You can help students master the art of "slanting" by arranging for them to write for a variety of readers: classmates, teachers, students in earlier grades, and parents. Be sure that each time you give an assignment, you include a designated target audience.

• **Choice:** While you will often need to specify the assignment, you can help students become independent and motivated writers by sometimes allowing them to choose the format and the content. For example, after teaching both the one-minute play and the fable, you might ask students to choose which format to use for their next writing assignment.

• **Curriculum:** Writing is a universal learning tool. It is best learned when integrated skillfully into all content areas. For example, students can review a book read for social studies when learning the book review format, and they can practice descriptive writing by documenting their thinking processes while solving math problems. This kind of cross-content strategy helps you do two jobs at once: deepen subject matter learning, and provide extra writing practice.

TEACH THE FORMAT

When students don't understand the structure and conventions of a format, problems occur. To avoid wasted time, lack of motivation, and inferior products, we use the following techniques for making sure students know what to do.

• **Provide models.** Recognizing a format's structure and elements does not stifle creativity. Originality relates to the content, not the form. Thus, if you want your students to write book reviews, first show them many reviews. Read them aloud, and have students read them to each other or read them silently. Ask students to find and share other examples. Later, list the key elements that students need to include when they compose their own reviews.

Where can you find models? For starters, one is given for each activity in this book. Other sources are: your reading text, books, magazines, and newspapers. *With their permission* we also save and use student work. You can, of course, create your own models. It takes only minutes and allows you to spot pitfalls that students might face. You'll then be ready to help students avoid common problems.

• **Offer step-by-step directions.** Experienced writers usually follow routines in creating their works. This does not mean that all novelists follow the same steps, or that all poets use the same method. There is no one right way to produce a type of writing. In fact, a sign of maturity is developing one's own method.

Still, a clear, ready-to-use recipe can be of value to students, especially at the start of a writing period, to help overcome inertia. Some students may want to follow every step; others may use a recipe only to address a problem. Highly intuitive students may never need the directions.

You will find a recipe for each assignment in this book. Feel free to reproduce them, modify them, or use them as starting points for creating your own tips.

• **Demonstrate steps you want students to follow.** Nothing is more memorable than watching an expert handle a task. By composing on the board or overhead and thinking aloud to let students follow your thought processes, you can teach many tasks, such as creating a lead paragraph or tagging dialogue. Rather than demonstrate everything, focus on skills that are new to students or particularly difficult.

KEEP ASSIGNMENTS SHORT

Young writers sometimes think that they have achieved something special by filling up page after page. But quantity has nothing to do with quality. A 10-page story that is trite and error-filled is bad writing, whereas a one-page story that is fresh and well-crafted is a work worth reading.

Successful writers often hone their skills on short forms, such as short stories and letters. Short assignments are effective because they put a premium on the keys to good writing:

- a big idea
- organization
- word choice
- well-made sentences
- interesting facts and examples
- careful revision

The short assignment also prepares writers for longer works, which are in fact written piece by piece. For example, novels consist of chapters, which are built of scenes, which grow from paragraphs. As Nobel-Prize-winner Claude Simon put it, "The big chore is always the same: how to begin a sentence, how to continue it, how to complete it."

For these reasons, and because short assignments promote sharing, this book's activities usually require only a few hundred words. This does not mean zipping through a task. With your guidance, students are more likely to spend time polishing their words when there are fewer words to polish.

Another plus is that students usually do a more thoughtful job of self-evaluating short pieces, and accepting feedback from others. (It's another example of "less being more.")

To help students grasp the creative potential of short pieces, read aloud classic examples, such as Aesop's fables. Some one-minute radio and TV public service announcements brilliantly illustrate the art of saying a lot in a small space. Poetry also teaches the same lesson.

Certainly, an occasional long assignment contributes to your program's balance. You'll see examples of these in the "Extra" section of the activities. But for the most part, if you rely on shorter pieces, students will progress faster to the ultimate goal: quality writing.

How to Teach Writing Without Going Crazy © 1998 Monday Morning Books, Inc.

GIVE USEFUL ASSIGNMENTS

To help students appreciate the value of writing, give them assignments that clearly help others. Toward that end, we've included a number of useful activities, such as the "Speech Introduction." But you can find many other "practical" writing opportunities in the school, such as:

• **Story hour:** Have students write stories and nonfiction pieces for younger children, and present this work to the intended audience via live visits to classroom or on video.

• **Classroom resources:** Invite students to create signs, posters, and learning center directions. As an ongoing project, students can contribute to a book of tips on solving story problems, illustrating posters, leading class meetings, developing experiments, telling stories, and handling classroom jobs. Such writing involves students in aiding classmates while creating their own learning environment.

• **Lectures:** Encourage students to write and deliver curriculum speeches that review topics that you already taught. For example, during a grammar unit, students might present lessons on the parts of speech, sentence types, punctuation marks, and capitalization rules. This assignment provides practice in a skill valued in school and on the job.

• **Answer service:** Have students use research to answer questions asked by younger kids, such as "Why does it rain?" To launch the project, your students might write a request-for-questions letter to the younger students.

• **Book reviews:** Ask the librarian if your students can review new library books. Publish the reviews in a binder in the library, on a bulletin board, or on the school's Web site.

• **Advice for incoming students:** At the end of the year, have students write letters to your future students with hints on how to do well during the year.

• **Learning logs:** End lessons by having students review what they learned. A useful review form is called "3, 2,1." Students list: three new or interesting ideas; two skills they practiced; and the one most vital idea or event of the day.

• **Student report cards:** For practice in self-evaluation, have students create report cards for themselves.

SHARPEN SKILLS WITH QUICK PRACTICES

Whenever students work on specific assignments, they simultaneously develop general writing skills, for example, organizing and editing. They also work on mechanics, such as punctuation and spelling.

However, most students need additional skill practice. We believe that the best way to provide it is via focused exercises that serve as warm-ups or transitions. Although brief, their intensity makes them efficient. They provide the same benefits athletes get when working on an element of a game, such as shooting free-throws.

One of the best-known examples is the "Daily Edit." The teacher (or a student) writes a defective sentence on the board. The sentence generally includes content and mechanics problems. The content problem can relate to a topic studied in class or to common knowledge:

> The moon is 400,000 Meters from Earth.

Students, working alone or with a partner, read the text and then write an edited version in their notebooks:

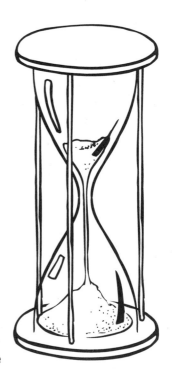

> The moon is 400,000 kilometers from Earth.

Students also explain the changes: "Don't capitalize measurements such as *inch* or *meters*. Correct the fact error: it's 400,000 kilometers, not 400,000 meters."

The teacher goes over the changes on the board as students check their work and make additional changes as needed.

You can create your own edits, focusing on problems found in your students' writing. There are also commercially published materials available. One of our favorites is *Ten-Minute Editing Skill Builders* (but maybe we're biased because we wrote it).

Virtually all skills can be developed through similar practices. You'll find many suggestions in part 2 of this book, and also in the Resources section.

DON'T BE THE ONLY READER

If you're the only reader of students' writing, you might give the message that only a teacher can appreciate a student's work. In reality, learning to write well requires writing for a variety of readers, and also responding to feedback from many perspectives. Even if you choose to read all papers closely, the following alternatives will provide the needed variety of readers that will give your students a more authentic writing experience.

Student interaction: Student writers can be helpful to one another. However, usually this does not happen without teacher guidance, encouragement, and structure. Before doing any peer editing or feedback, be sure the guidelines are clearly established:

> Read the piece (or part of it).
> Tell what is strong about it.
> Ask questions.
> Make suggestions.

Be clear that there is no room for making fun of anyone's writing. This framework should be demonstrated by the teacher and a student writer and practiced in pairs independently before students are expected to function on their own. Three types of interaction are:

• *Editing buddies*: Use random drawings to assign weekly "editing buddies." Review the criteria in the assignment so that students will know what to comment on. Usually, more emphasis should be put on content issues than mechanics.

• *Writers' groups*: Many professionals rely on groups for feedback. (See Resources for tips on this kind of sharing.)

• *Cross-age reading*: This is especially valuable with expository forms. Trying to make subjects clear for younger readers provides realistic practice for such skills as word choice and choosing appropriate examples. Many activities in this book are well-suited to cross-age publishing.

Focused feedback: Receiving a great many feedback comments on a draft can be overwhelming to a student writer. To avoid this it's sometimes best to focus on one or a few issues. For example, if an assignment called for students to include three unusual facts in a research paper, you might limit your feedback to that issue. At the same time, you could arrange for students to share their papers in small groups. This way, they'll get feedback on all aspects of the work.

INVOLVE PARENTS

To help parents become a valuable resource for your program, explain to them in a jargon-free way your goals, methods, and standards. Invite them to visit your room and view works in progress and finished works. Discuss the writing process, and listen to their questions. With this foundation, they'll more likely succeed with tasks such as:

Reading aloud: When students listen to literature, they develop a feel for language that is vital for sentence writing, punctuation, and editing. To encourage this activity, give parents a reading list that focuses on the formats and skills you're working on in class. The more varied the list in terms of writing types and content, the better. Also, suggest that parents ask their children read aloud their own writing, including early drafts and polished versions.

So what was it like in the old days, growing up without a computer?

Talking: Talking and writing are closely connected. Through conversations over meals and during other family activities, students are likely to become more curious about the world, leading them to questions and ideas.

Sharing knowledge: For example, when writing essays comparing life two decades ago with life today, students can brainstorm questions about events, music, fashion, and so on, and then interview their parents.

Collaborating: Experiment with writing partnerships:
• Rhymed poetry (couplets): The parent writes the first line, and the student writes the second line.
• Instruction manual: The parent demonstrates a skill, such as cooking or woodworking, and the student writes about it.
• Group story: The student writes the opening paragraph. The parent writes the second paragraph, and so on.
• Two-person play: The parent writes the lines for one character, while the student writes the lines for the other.

Editing: Invite parents to comment on their children's work. (See the next page for sample guidelines.)

Proofreading: The parent notes errors in the margin. For example, if there's a missing word, the parent writes "missing word." The parent does NOT correct the text. That is the student's job. The student uses the proofreading notes to find errors and make corrections. A list of proofreading marks is found in the Resources section of this book.

How to Teach Writing Without Going Crazy © 1998 Monday Morning Books, Inc.

Sample Letter

Dear Parent,

   Most published writers work with editors. These are "trial readers" who offer constructive feedback. The following steps are designed to help you play this vital role for your child. Because we are practicing the same routine in class, this procedure should be familiar to your child.

1. Before starting, have writing implements handy.

2. Ask your child to briefly describe the lesson. You can expect an explanation such as:
- "The idea was to describe a character in a story."
- "We were learning to write business letters."
- "I was to write a rhyming poem for young children."

3. Have your child read the writing aloud to you. Make notes that will help you remember any thoughts, but try not to interrupt the reading.

4. When your child is done reading, first point out parts that you liked. Instead of a vague comment such as, "It was good," try something more exact, for example, "Your story's ending surprised me," or "I had a similar experience one time." Be careful not to offer too many comments because that can be overwhelming.

5. Deal with problems by making constructive suggestions. Again, be specific. Instead of "I didn't like the middle part," you might say, "The middle confused me. Maybe it would be clearer if you gave an example."
   Also, although spelling and other technical matters are important, don't focus only on them. Ideas and content are even more vital. Remember, the goal of writing is to communicate.

6. Do not take over. You may know exactly what will solve the problem, but if you solve it, your child won't benefit. For the best results, point out problems orally or by making notes on the margin.

7. Be patient. The road to writing mastery is long. No single assignment is decisive. What we're looking for is steady improvement.

TEACH THE WRITING PROCESS

Writing well requires handling a variety of jobs, such as getting ideas, organizing, drafting, and editing. These tasks, which comprise the writing process, are "universals." They come into play no matter what the form. For example, ideas are needed whether the assignment is to write a poem, a letter, a story, or an essay.

There are two ways to help students master the writing process. One approach is to teach it explicitly by defining and practicing the tasks. The other method is to have students learn about the process while writing assignments.

Which approach should be used? We think both. We find it useful to start by teaching the students the tasks using a seven-part model. (See pages 18-31 for details.) Their initial learning can then be reinforced by specific practices used as warm-ups for the writing period, and by feedback given while students work on specific assignments.

We like using a seven-sided model to illustrate the writing process. This conveys the reality that the writing process is nonlinear and recursive. For example, a writer may get an idea for a new project while doing research for an old one. Another example: When drafting a piece, a writer might realize that more research is required.

Creating a bulletin board of this model provides constant visual reinforcement of the concepts. It also serves as a map students can use to track their progress in creating a piece of writing.

Writing Process Model

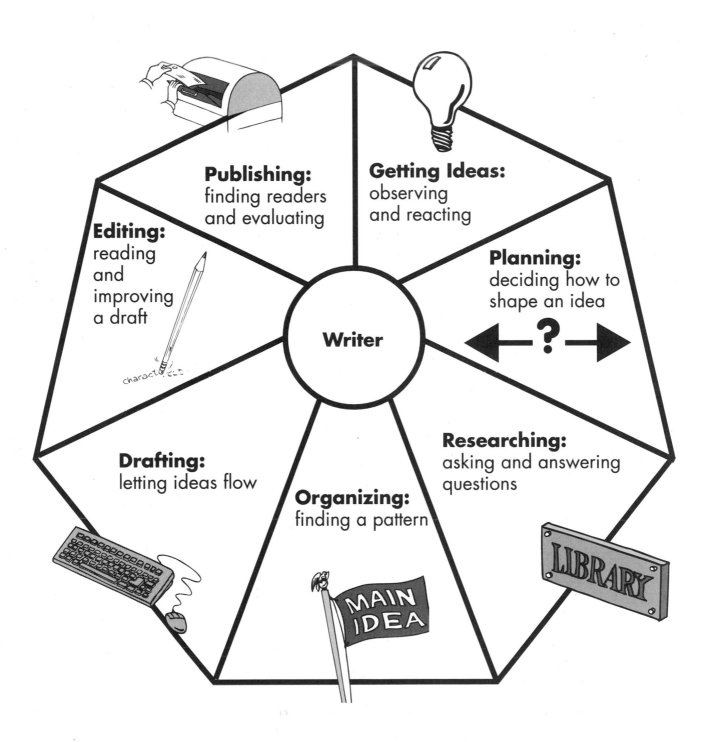

Publishing: finding readers and evaluating

Getting Ideas: observing and reacting

Editing: reading and improving a draft

Planning: deciding how to shape an idea

Writer

Drafting: letting ideas flow

Researching: asking and answering questions

Organizing: finding a pattern

GETTING IDEAS

Getting ideas is like what happens when a grain of sand enters an oyster's shell. The oyster reacts to this stimulus by forming a pearl. In the same way, when a person notices and reacts to a stimulus, this event—getting an idea—can eventually lead to creating something even more valuable than a pearl, for example, a poem, an essay, a play, or a story.

The following practices are meant to help students become more prolific idea collectors, who value their own experiences as writing topics.

Keeping an idea journal: Ideas are slippery, and easy to forget. That's why most artists, inventors, writers, and scientists write down their thoughts often in a pocket notebook or computer file. In the classroom, have students maintain idea notebooks or sections in their language arts binders. Each entry should be dated. If some priming is needed, suggest idea starters. On various days, ask students to list 10 (or some such number):
• skills that you have
• people you'd want with you on a trip to Mars
• places you know something about
• words that mean something special to you
• experiences you're glad you had...or wish you hadn't had
• inventions you hope will be invented in your lifetime
Hint: NEVER grade journals.

Observing: Regularly give students observation tasks.
• Describe something in detail—a watch, the back of the hand, breathing, etc. For fun, students can pretend that they are describing the thing to someone from the distant past.
• From memory, describe a familiar room. Later, while in the room, add at least three details to the description.
• Observe something in a new way: watch a favorite TV program with the sound turned off, listen to a TV show without looking at it, view a familiar object upside down, use a magnifying glass to look at something.

Listening to idea people: Invite writers, inventors, artists, teachers, and other thinkers to your room to discuss how they get ideas for their work.

Brainstorming: Writing teacher Gabriele Rico (*Writing the Natural Way*) advises that the best way to have one good idea is to first generate many ideas. The following activities encourage such "fluent" thinking:
- Other uses: List many uses of an object, such as a shoe:

      a doorstop   a dried-flower vase   a hammer
      a toy boat   a pencil holder   a puppet
- Product naming: List 10 names for a bicycle shop, etc.
- Titling: Generate several titles for a piece of writing. For example, three titles for a biography of an uncle might be:

      My Favorite Uncle
      My Daredevil Uncle
      Uncle Somebody
- Naming characters: When naming a story's protagonist, brainstorm several, then choose the best and explain why.
- Predicting: Before reaching the climax of a story, have students brainstorm endings and explain which they think is the best.
- Finding synonyms: See how many ways kids, working alone or in groups, can express the meaning of a word like *friend*: pal, helper, someone who likes you, etc.
- Using words many ways: Write a word with multiple meanings on the board, and see how many ways students can use it, for example: *fly*.

      A fly is buzzing in the room.
      The batter hit a fly ball.
      I'm going to fly in an airplane.

PLANNING

An idea is just a starting point for a piece of writing. The next step is deciding what to make of the idea. Will it become a funny poem or a serious essay or a children's book? Sometimes students will be making these decisions, Other times, the teacher will assign the format and its treatment. Either way, planning a piece involves dealing with the following issues:

• *Purpose*: A work can have several goals, but it's best to have one main goal in mind.

• *Scope*: This relates to how much of the subject is covered. For example, a chess article might cover all aspects of the game, or it might deal only with the opening moves.

• *Format*: One idea can become a poem, a letter, or something different.

• *Audience*: Who the writing is for affects word choice, examples, average sentence length, and other writing issues.

• *Length*: While some formats have a natural length, with many others the number of words must be determined.

• *Point of view*: Options are: first person, second person, and third person.

• *Tone*: A writer has many voices, such as neutral, angry, silly, bold, and sarcastic.

The following activities can help students become familiar with the issues involved in planning a piece of writing.

Purpose: Have students choose a subject, and write titles that suggest different writing purposes. For example, if the subject is bicycles, titles might be:

> How to Repair a Bicycle (teaching a skill)
> Three Reasons to Wear a Helmet (changing behavior)
> The Joy of Bicycling (description)

Scope: Have students describe a picture in about 50 words. Now change the *focus* by identifying a small part of the picture and have them describe the area in the same number of words. Try the same activity using a personal experience. In 50 words students describe events they experienced, for example, a family outing. Then they choose one part of the event and describe it in the same number of words.

Format: To help students distinguish between form and content, give students a poem and have them translate its message into the form of a story or essay. Try the same activity but have students use their own material. For example, a visit to relatives could be described in a poem, a short play, a story, or a speech.

Audience: Give students a nonfiction article written at their reading level, and have them translate it into terms that a young child could understand.

For a more personal exercise in slanting, have students write imaginary letters to themselves when they were five years old.

Length: To help students understand that it's possible to present any subject in more or less detail, give students a newspaper article or short story and have them rewrite the piece using half as many words. Then have them expand it to twice the number of words as the original.

Try the activity using student writing. For example, students describe an object in 50 words, then compress the description into 25 words, and expand it to 200 words.

Point of view: Gives students a story, and have them retell it in a different point of view. If it's first person, they could tell it in second or third person.

For a personal version of this activity, have students write short autobiographies, then rewrite them in the third person, referring to themselves as *he* or *she*.

Tone: Find an angry letter to the editor, and have students rewrite it in a calmer tone.

For a more creative experience, students can write two versions of a 60-second commercial: one serious, one silly. Each version should convey the same information.

RESEARCHING

Researching does not begin with reference books. It starts when someone recognizes that he or she doesn't understand something. This realization leads to asking questions. The questions lead to the search for answers.

Experienced writers know three ways to find answers: using information packages (books, magazines, Web sites, etc.); observing first hand; and asking people (via interviews or surveys). Each method requires special skills. For example, getting information from a book often calls for paraphrasing; eyewitness observing may involve making sketches.

Whatever the source, when in doubt, the careful researcher double-checks the facts by trying a second source, or a third.

Make sure students understand that research can play a role in any type of writing. It has an obvious function in nonfiction assignments, such as the report. But it can be equally useful in so-called creative forms. For example, novelists often spend time gathering information needed to create realistic scenes, settings, and characters.

The following activities are meant to help students enjoy research as well as become adept at it.

Asking questions: Give students a subject and have them brainstorm as many questions as they can about it. This might be done solo or in small groups. For example, if the subject is rollerblades, questions might be:
    Who invented rollerblades?
    How popular is rollerblading?
    How dangerous is rollerblading?
    What would make rollerblading safer?
    Who is the best rollerblader in the world?

Creating story settings: Have students research locations for short stories, and then use the information they found when actually writing their stories. An example would be a story set in the gardens of Versailles.

Going on scavenger hunts: Draw up a list of questions and have students, solo or in small groups, find the answers. In most cases, allow students to use all sources, but sometimes focus on a single source, for example, "All answers must come from newspaper articles" or "All articles must come from Web sites" or "All answers must come from experts whom you queried." Each answer must be accompanied by the source.

Confirming information: Give students a newspaper article and have them find a source to confirm each important fact.

Taking notes while interviewing: Invite an expert to the classroom (another teacher, an administrator, an older student) and have students take notes while everyone has a chance to pose questions. Later, compare the completeness of the notes.

Taking notes while observing: Have students use drawings as well as word pictures to describe ordinary objects (buttons, fruit, coins, bolts) and unusual objects (for example, cooking implements they won't be familiar with).

Paraphrasing printed material: Make sure students understand that paraphrasing means "putting ideas in one's own words." Explain that sometimes we copy material word for word (for example, to get an excerpt for a review). In general, though, paraphrasing forces us to think more deeply about the material and understand it better.
• As a warm-up, give students a sentence and have them express the same idea using mostly—or entirely—different words. Proverbs work well for this task:

> Original: Two heads are better than one.
> Paraphrase: A pair of thinkers may come up with a
> better idea or plan than a single thinker.

• To practice realistic paraphrasing, give students a text of about 100 words, then on a separate paper write notes using no more than 20 words. After you collect the original text, have students use their notes to "reconstitute" the material in their own words. The key to successful paraphrasing is not looking at the original while writing the new version. If the original is in plain sight, it will interfere with the process of thinking about the ideas and finding a way to express them.

Paraphrasing is not learned in a day. This practice should be repeated frequently.

ORGANIZING

Many people find organizing difficult, whether it's organizing an essay or organizing their lives. (Think of all those companies selling closet organizing systems!)

A simple analogy can help kids grasp this process. When packing a suitcase for a trip you need to:
- Collect all the items you might bring.
- Decide what to take—and what to leave behind.
- Group items to be taken into groups—socks, shirts, etc.
- Decide where to put each group in the suitcase.

Writers go through the same organizing steps. They:
- Review the materials collected when getting ideas, planning, and researching.
- Decide what belongs and what doesn't. Trying to work in an item that doesn't fit usually creates problems. It's better to put it aside for another project.
- Choose an organizing pattern—such as chronological order—that fits the material. (Several classic patterns appear on the next page.) Readers stay on track when they recognize a familiar structure encountered in other works. Then they can concentrate on the material.
- Arrange the material. Outlining can be useful. But some writers find outlines too abstract and prefer more concrete methods such as using diagrams and other graphic organizers, or physically moving around note cards or piles of materials.

The following practices can help students gain confidence in handling this vital step in the writing process.

Brainstorming subtopics: Give students titles and have them brainstorm subtopics. For example, the title "Why I Like Spaghetti" might suggest the following topics:
    1. The name is fun to say.
    2. The noodles looks like fun on the plate.
    3. It's a challenge to eat a spaghetti meal.
Other titles to use for this practice:
- Foods I Hate
- Waking Up in the Morning
- The Daily Journey to School
- What Makes a Good Book
- The Differences Between Hearing and Seeing
- Secrets

Practicing patterns: Have students use a familiar organizational pattern to organize parts of a subject:
• Chronological: Describe a common activity in a few steps, for example, getting dressed or throwing a Frisbee.
• Alphabetical: List the items in your room alphabetically.
• Overview + details: List subtopics that support an idea:
• Ranking: Rank five favorites in any category (toys, articles of clothing, authors, places). End with the top item.
• Spatial: Describe your head from top to bottom.

Analyzing works: Give students a short piece, such as a news article, a chapter in a science text, a fable, or a letter. Have them use outlining or diagramming to identify the pattern and key points. Then discuss the structure.

Playing the In/Out Game: For practice in selecting or rejecting material, list several related items on the board:
• orange   • basketball
• golf ball   • soccer ball
Ask students to exclude one item and give a reason for doing so. Then, ask them to exclude a second item, and again give a reason. Return to the original list and have students add another item, and explain why.
        Note: Organizing is creative. There is no one right answer to what should be included or excluded. What matters is having a reason for the choice.

Editing outlines: Write an outline on the board and have students try to improve it. The outline might be missing an obvious topic, or the topics might be in a confusing order.

Writing from outlines: To help students focus on structure have them write pieces using ready-made outlines, such as:
        How to Brush Your Teeth
        1. Assemble materials
        2. Prepare brush
        3. Brush
        4. Rinse
        5. Cleanup
Students could write the outlines and swap with partners.

Outlining finished assignments: When students have completed a piece, sometimes ask them to outline their work. This use of outlining can help writers discover problems of organization.

DRAFTING

Noted editor Max Perkins advised young writers to "get it down on paper, and then we'll see what we can make of it." Easier said than done. Many students find it difficult to get started or to write freely once they do get started. This is often caused by a fear of making mistakes.

Those who understand the writing process don't have that worry. They know that after drafting, they will enter the editing phase, where they can improve the draft. In fact, savvy writers (at least those working on paper) leave wide margins and skip lines so they have room to make changes.

The activities below can help students learn to hear their inner voices and to capture the flow of ideas and images.

Timed writing: The goal is to practice writing freely for a set period. A minute is good for a first effort; eventually you might expand it to two or three minutes. To help students get started, post an optional word or picture prompt. (See next page for examples.) Of course, students should feel free to write on their own topics if they prefer. Two other "rules" for the activity:
1) Students should keep their pencils or pens moving.
2) The material should not be graded or even read by the teacher unless the student wants to share it. The goal is to let the words out, not to evaluate them.

Taking dictation: Drafting is like taking dictation. To practice this process, read aloud a passage, and have students write it as they hear it. You might remind them of a specific issue, for example, starting a new paragraph whenever a different character talks.

Group composition: Divide the class into pairs or small groups. Each student writes the first paragraph of an essay on a topic that everyone knows about. The paper is then passed to another student who writes a second paragraph, and then passes it on. This activity gives students practice in reading a manuscript and then adding to it.

Experimenting with leads: A powerful opening sentence or paragraph can create momentum. Pick one of the classic types of leads and have students draft a paragraph using it. For example, describe something you did yesterday, but make the first sentence a quotation.

Classic Types of Leads
- Startling fact
- Setting (time/place)
- Character description
- Action
- Question
- Quotation
- Definition
- Command to the reader
- Summary or main idea

TImed-writing Starters

• Choose an activity that you like (watching TV, rollerblading, eating spaghetti) and explain why you like it.

• Choose someone real or from a story that you might like to be—or a day or forever—and explain why.

• If you had to be some object, what would it be and why would you choose it? (car, bicycle, key, book, toenail clipper, etc.)

• Pick any two things that come together in your mind, and explain how they are alike and different. (TV/radio; books/movies; school/home; day/night; sun/moon; water/soda; summer/winter; friend/enemy).

• Pick a job that you would like to have and explain why.

• Pick a place that you would like to visit and explain why.

• Tell why you think it would be good—or bad if—teachers were replaced by robots.

• Describe how your life would be changed if a common object no longer existed. (TV, radio, paper, computers).

Let the ideas flow

• If you could read other people's minds without their knowing it, would you want that power? Why or why not?

• What do you think is the most important invention in the world? Explain why.

• If you could change one thing in the world, what would it be and why?

• Name a skill that you don't have but that you'd like to develop, and explain why you'd like to have that skill.

• Tell why it would—or wouldn't—be a good idea if everyone in the world spoke the same language.

EDITING

Editing is also called "revising" or "polishing." By any name, if young writers are not taught the importance of this step, they often dislike it and associate it with unneeded work. Experienced writers, on the other hand, usually love editing, which gives them a chance to improve their work.

To help students gain a positive understanding of editing, explain that it's like what happens when getting dressed. After putting on clothes, you look in a mirror to check things out. The mirror provides a fresh perspective. If a garment doesn't look right, you can put on something else. At the same time, the mirror shows you the positive aspects of your appearance. Next, you may ask someone for comments. The person's observations give another opportunity to set things right.

Editing a manuscript works the same way. To get a fresh perspective, the writer briefly puts the manuscript aside. (This is the reason for not waiting until the last minute to do an assignment.) Next, the writer becomes his or her *first reader*— enjoying the good parts and making changes of three sorts: content (ideas, facts, imagery); wording (preciseness, freshness), and mechanics (spelling, punctuation, grammar). After this "self-editing," the smart writer usually seeks additional comments from friends or a professional editor. The goal always is to improve the work.

The following practices can help students learn to critically read their work, gracefully accept feedback, and make needed changes.

Editing mock manuscripts: Many students at first are defensive about changing their own work. That's why it's easier to develop editing skills by practicing on teacher-created sample manuscripts. These mock manuscripts contain problems of content, wording, and mechanics that students discover and correct. It is helpful to have the students work in pairs because their discussion as they make corrections is often clarifying. For best results, have students justify the changes they have made. One important learning from this practice is that there may be many ways to edit a piece. Note: The more often the students do this practice, the better they'll get at it.

Responding to comments: Often, a teacher writes helpful notes on papers, but students ignore them. Thus the teacher's time is wasted, and the student learns nothing. Editorial notes are meaningless unless a writer reads them and uses those that make sense. To provide students with practice in reading and using written feedback, give students mock manuscripts that contain feedback written in the margins or attached. These "mock editing notes" should resemble the kind of feedback you would give students, or that you hope students will learn to give each other. (A list of traditional proofreader's symbols is provided in the Resources section.)

Guided self-editing. When students work on actual assignments, they should have a chance in class to edit their work. However, because we don't assume that students will know what to look for, we generally guide them, especially early in the year. We do so by listing the points they should check. For example, if they have written a short story, we might ask them to check and fix, if necessary, the following:
• title: Is it focused and fresh (not "A Story" but "The Nasty Sock").
• setting: Is it clearly pictured? Does it relate to the action?
• Dialogue: Is every speech meaningful? That is, can the writer give a reason for including it?

As for **mechanics**, we naturally want every finished work to be free of spelling, punctuation, and other technical errors. We have found, however, that students will become more focused on mechanics if we provide a focus. For example, during the guided editing session, we might tell students to "Be extra careful about homonym errors." We might be even more precise and say, "Check every its/it's to make sure none is mixed up."

Table reading: In many professional writing programs, teachers arrange for "table readings." Working in small groups, each student reads aloud the draft of a short manuscript, or an excerpt from a longer piece. (In some cases, a fellow student does the reading.) Other students listen, take notes, and then provide helpful feedback using the criteria spelled out when the assignment was given. For example, if a story's main conflict was to be introduced on
page one, listeners will note whether or not that happened.

The idea of reading the text aloud puts the attention on content (ideas, descriptions, facts, flow) rather than on mechanics, which will be dealt with separately. (For guidelines on peer editing, see Resources.)

PUBLISHING

Publishing might seem like a trivial—if ego-boosting—step. It involves cleaning up the lettering, adding art, and generally dressing up a work for the public. But this step is actually profound. It is the time for evaluating and looking ahead to new challenges. These tasks can be powerful learning experiences.

The following practices are meant to help students treat their finished work with the respect it deserves, and to use it as a springboard for further learning.

Self-evaluating: Students aren't born knowing how to self-evaluate. Fortunately, there is an easy-to-use structure for handling this task (see next page). If this step is new to your class, demonstrate how to use the framework by evaluating something that you wrote. We believe that students should evaluate each important assignment *before* handing it in. Their efforts will make them more open to your comments, and eventually they'll come up with useful insights.

Self-grading: If grades are required, have students practice with a point system so that they will be able to grade themselves before the teacher does. For example, students get 10 points if all format elements are included,

Looking ahead: Successful writers view each piece as a learning experience, and usually are eager to try again. This is true of professionals who write best-selling novels, but it's also true of amateurs, like those who write letters to the editor. That is why we include a space on the framework for writers to think about their next steps.

Preparing for sharing: It is not enough to put student work "out there." The work must be ready for reading. Readers deserve excellence. Equally important, you will be judged by the work that leaves your room. If your students put up a bulletin board in the hallway, it should be worth stopping by and reading. One possibility is to make sure it is entirely free of mistakes, or if the work has not been edited for every possible item, include a note, such as "Work in Progress."

How to Teach Writing Without Going Crazy © 1998 Monday Morning Books, Inc.

Self-evaluation Framework

Author's name_____ Type of work_____

Title of work_____

Criteria (given at the time of the assignment)

_____

_____

What I think is best about this work:

_____

_____

Parts that needed more work:

_____

_____

Lessons I learned while doing this assignment:

_____

_____

What I would have done differently:

_____

_____

Future project I'd like to work on using this format:

_____

_____

DESCRIPTIVE WRITING BASICS

The goal of descriptive writing is to send a picture from the author's mind to the reader's. The activity involves the following steps:

Get the picture. The writer first needs a clear picture of the subject. This sometimes involves observing the subject. Other times, it requires imagining the subject.

Choose important details. Too many details may overwhelm the reader. For example, in describing a beach, there's no need to say exactly how many grains of sand there are. The trick is choosing the most important details.

Find the right words. Naming the subject isn't enough. The writer must use words that *show* the subject. Usually these will be words that label information from the senses: colors, textures, shapes, sounds, smells. It's also important to use words that make sense to the intended reader. *Plateau* may create a clear picture for some people, but young children may not understand what it means.

Organize the information. A description can start by naming the subject: "There's a beautiful garden in my neighborhood." But it could also start with details. Another possibility is to begin with a comparison. For example, to describe a highway interchange, a writer might say that the roads "look like tangled spaghetti noodles." Then, specific details would be added to complete the picture.

We have a new kitten. It's a calico. She's batting a ball of yarn back and forth, and has got it tangled around her head.

Evaluating Descriptive Writing

The following points can be used when editing or judging descriptive writing.

1. Is the subject clearly defined? This can be done by including an introductory sentence at the beginning of the description, for example, "We have the most unusual garden in the world." But it is also possible to explain what the subject is simply by using well-chosen details.

2. Is there enough information to allow the reader to "see" the picture? Often the details will be visual, covering color, size, and shapes. But descriptive writing can also include information related to other senses, for example, touch and smell.

3. Are the details presented in an orderly way that makes them easy to grasp? If the details are just thrown at the reader in no order, the result can be confusion. That's why writers often have a plan, for example, starting at a distance to give the "big" picture, and then moving in closer. Or starting at the top of the subject and moving down.

4. Does the wording fit the audience? Older readers or those who know a lot about a subject will be able to handle more advanced language. Younger readers, or those who know little about the subject, will need more basic information.

5. Are the comparisons fresh? If the writer uses a comparison it should not be a cliche. That's a comparison most people have already heard. An example of a cliche would be to describe someone as being "busy as a bee."

6. Does the description have a real purpose? For example, if a story contains a detailed description of a bicycle, the bicycle should play a role in the story. Otherwise, the description might distract or bore readers.

CHARACTER SKETCH

A character is a person, an animal, or a human-like figure (such as a ghost) found in a story or drama. A character sketch tells what the character is like. This description could include the character's appearance, personality, and habits.

DIRECTIONS:

1. List a few familiar characters. They can come from books, movies, plays, and TV shows.

2. Choose one character to write about. It could be a hero, a villain, or even a minor but interesting character.

3. List words and phrases that the character brings to mind. Think about:
• physical qualities such as size, shape, clothing, and age
• actions such as the way the character moves, talks, laughs, and solves problems

4. Write a short essay that describes the character in detail. The essay might be one paragraph or a few paragraphs. It's OK to retell part of the story while describing the character, but keep the focus on the character, not the plot.
• Start by mentioning the story that the character is from.
• To organize the main part of the essay, you might group physical qualities in one paragraph and actions in another.
• End by explaining what's most important or memorable about the character.

5. Share the sketch with someone who knows about the character. Ask for suggestions that might make the sketch clearer or more interesting.

EXTRA:
Before writing an original story, try drafting character sketches for the main characters. Doing so can make the characters seem more real, and may also suggest details for the story.

How to Teach Writing Without Going Crazy © 1998 Monday Morning Books, Inc.

Model Character Sketch

King Kong

King Kong is a gorilla who is the main character in a 1933 movie titled *King Kong*.

The first things you notice about King Kong are his size and strength. He's so big that he can hold a person in his hand. He's so strong that he can wrestle with and defeat a Tyrannosaurus Rex, and also toss around railway cars. Kong's voice is also as loud as thunder.

Kong is a violent creature who terrifies the people living on his island in the Pacific Ocean. His violence shows even more when he's brought to New York City and put on display. After he snaps the huge chains that hold him, he wrecks the theater and then causes major damage in the city. During this commotion, many people are killed.

But the real surprise is that Kong has a tender part of his personality. Early in the movie, he falls in love with a young woman named Ann. (Most people who have seen the movie don't remember her name. Instead, they refer to her by the name of the actress, Fay Wray, who is most famous for her loud screams as Kong chases her.)

At the end of the movie, Kong carries Ann to the top of the Empire State Building. There, he is badly wounded by bullets from fighter planes. When the gorilla realizes that he is about to die, he gently puts Ann in a safe place so that she won't tumble off the skyscraper with him. This shows that he has the ability to care about someone, and not just do destructive acts.

In fact, throughout the movie, Kong causes problems only when he is attacked. He does not go after people just to hurt them. If people stayed out of his way, he probably wouldn't cause them harm.

King Kong is both violent and loving. This combination makes him a memorable character.

EYEWITNESS REPORT

Knowledge often comes from observation. This is true in the sciences—think of the Hubble Telescope—and in the arts.

DIRECTIONS:

1. Pick a subject to observe. It could be a person or group of people, an object, or a place.

2. Decide when to observe and for how long. For example, you might plan to spend five minutes observing kindergartners playing during recess.

3. Gather observation materials. These usually include writing implements for taking notes. In some cases, you'll also want a tool. For example, a magnifying glass would be useful when observing an insect or some other small thing.

4. While observing, be ready to use more than one sense. For example, sounds may enrich a description of a forest. In addition to words, try making drawings.

5. Draft the report. Decide whether to label the observer with the pronoun "I" or with a neutral title such as "the reporter." Include the following parts:
• A descriptive title: In a science report, be specific, for example, "Changes in the Moon's Position During February."
• An introduction that sets the scene: This might explain why the subject was chosen.
• The observations: If the report deals with a subject that changes during the observation, include notes about the time so readers can tell how quickly the changes happened.
• A conclusion: This might sum up what was learned.

6. Share the report with a trial reader. Ask for feedback that would make it clearer. For example, the reader could let you know if the descriptive words are specific enough. Later, polish the text and invite others to read it.

EXTRA:

Describe a TV commercial or a TV show as if the actions were happening for real. Try using the present tense, for example, "A red car splashes through a puddle and then starts crying as if it were a person. The car says..."

EYEWITNESS REPORT

Knowledge often comes from observation. This is true in the sciences—think of the Hubble Telescope—and in the arts.

DIRECTIONS:

1. Pick a subject to observe. It could be a person or group of people, an object, or a place.

2. Decide when to observe and for how long. For example, you might plan to spend five minutes observing kindergartners playing during recess.

3. Gather observation materials. These usually include writing implements for taking notes. In some cases, you'll also want a tool. For example, a magnifying glass would be useful when observing an insect or some other small thing.

4. While observing, be ready to use more than one sense. For example, sounds may enrich a description of a forest. In addition to words, try making drawings.

5. Draft the report. Decide whether to label the observer with the pronoun "I" or with a neutral title such as "the reporter." Include the following parts:
• A descriptive title: In a science report, be specific, for example, "Changes in the Moon's Position During February."
• An introduction that sets the scene: This might explain why the subject was chosen.
• The observations: If the report deals with a subject that changes during the observation, include notes about the time so readers can tell how quickly the changes happened.
• A conclusion: This might sum up what was learned.

6. Share the report with a trial reader. Ask for feedback that would make it clearer. For example, the reader could let you know if the descriptive words are specific enough. Later, polish the text and invite others to read it.

EXTRA:
Describe a TV commercial or a TV show as if the actions were happening for real. Try using the present tense, for example, "A red car splashes through a puddle and then starts crying as if it were a person. The car says..."

Model Character Sketch

King Kong

King Kong is a gorilla who is the main character in a 1933 movie titled *King Kong*.

The first things you notice about King Kong are his size and strength. He's so big that he can hold a person in his hand. He's so strong that he can wrestle with and defeat a Tyrannosaurus Rex, and also toss around railway cars. Kong's voice is also as loud as thunder.

Kong is a violent creature who terrifies the people living on his island in the Pacific Ocean. His violence shows even more when he's brought to New York City and put on display. After he snaps the huge chains that hold him, he wrecks the theater and then causes major damage in the city. During this commotion, many people are killed.

But the real surprise is that Kong has a tender part of his personality. Early in the movie, he falls in love with a young woman named Ann. (Most people who have seen the movie don't remember her name. Instead, they refer to her by the name of the actress, Fay Wray, who is most famous for her loud screams as Kong chases her.)

At the end of the movie, Kong carries Ann to the top of the Empire State Building. There, he is badly wounded by bullets from fighter planes. When the gorilla realizes that he is about to die, he gently puts Ann in a safe place so that she won't tumble off the skyscraper with him. This shows that he has the ability to care about someone, and not just do destructive acts.

In fact, throughout the movie, Kong causes problems only when he is attacked. He does not go after people just to hurt them. If people stayed out of his way, he probably wouldn't cause them harm.

King Kong is both violent and loving. This combination makes him a memorable character.

Model Self-portrait

If my bicycle were alive, it might describe itself like this.

I'm Not Just Any Bicycle

During the school day if the weather is warm, you can usually find me in the bicycle cage at Jordan Junior High. Although there will be at least a hundred other two-wheelers there, I'm easy to find. You just have to know what to look for.

Like most of the other bicycles, I have thin tires, but mine will be nearly flat. That's because my owner, whose name I will not mention, never remembers to pump them up. Sometimes, as we roll along, people will yell out, "Your tires are flat." I never say anything. Why should I?

You'd think my owner would feel uncomfortable riding on almost-airless tires. He isn't. That's because he bought an extra-soft seat filled with foam rubber.

He attached lights and a large reflector to the back of the seat, which I think is a good idea because sometimes it's dark when we go home. A few other bikes also have this kind of safety equipment, but I think I'm the only one with a bell and a horn. Both of these noise makers work well. I didn't really need two of them, but my owner must think it's neat to sometimes honk and other times ring.

Maybe that is funny, but the mud that's all over my frame isn't. I haven't been bathed in such a long time, you can hardly see the red stripes that decorate my frame. I'm probably the muddiest bike in town. The only time I get even a little bit clean is when it rains.

You can see by the rust on some of my metal parts that my owner doesn't believe in wiping me off when we get home. He'll even leave me outside at times, but luckily his parents usually make him go back outside and put me into the nice, warm garage.

SNAPSHOT BIOGRAPHY

It is impossible to describe all of a person's life. One way to focus on a few important parts is for the biographer to imagine taking photographs of the subject.

DIRECTIONS:

1. Choose a familiar subject. It could be a friend, a relative, a neighbor, or someone from the community.

2. List at least three photographs that could show important moments or events in the subject's life. These are not real photographs, but ones that can be imagined.

3. Write a caption for each imaginary photograph. The captions should take the form of short paragraphs. Two or three sentences will usually be enough. Information that would not be seen in the photograph can be used, for example, names of people or places.

4. Draft the biography. Write a descriptive title, followed by a brief introduction.

5. Share the biography with someone who doesn't know your subject. Ask the reader to describe his or her impression of the person you wrote about. This might give clues for improving the biography.

6. Polish the biography. You might then give it to the person you wrote about.

EXTRA:

Write a snapshot biography about a historical figure based on research, or about a character in a movie or book.

Model Snapshot Biography

My Mother in Six Photos

Whenever I complain that I have a lot to do, I think of my mother, who is a lot busier than I am. Here are some of the activities that take up her time.

Helping a Customer Choose a Party Dress: My mother opened a clothing store eight years ago. She loves helping people find just the right things to wear. My mother also enjoys traveling to many cities to find products to sell in her shop.

Cooking Dinner: Although Mom works long hours six days a week, she prepares dinner most nights. She says cooking relaxes her. She looks at cooking as if it were an art, and takes cooking classes whenever she has time. She also owns a large collection of cookbooks.

Reading a News Magazine: Mom is interested in knowing about what's happening all around the world. She says she became interested in current events when she was in high school and a member of the debating team. Although people come to her store to buy clothes, they also seem to enjoy talking to Mom about the news.

Using the Computer: Many nights, Mom will spend an hour or more at the computer. She does not play games, however. She uses the machine to manage her bank account and other business matters.

Reading a Mystery: Mom usually can figure out who did the crime long before she reaches the last page. She says she learns nothing important by reading this kind of book, but she says this type of book helps balance the kind of thinking she has to do in order to keep her business going.

VIGNETTE

A vignette is a detailed description of a real event. Unlike a fictional story, a vignette usually doesn't have a surprise ending.

DIRECTIONS:

1. Choose an important incident. It can be something dramatic—for example, being on an airplane that has engine trouble—or it can be something more ordinary yet important, such as losing something.

2. Before writing about the incident, visualize it. Try to see it unfolding from beginning to end. Recall the emotion or emotions that were part of it. In addition to visual images, think about sounds including words that were spoken.

3. Draft the vignette. Give careful attention to the beginning. Writers often start with a sentence that tells the reader what to expect, for example: "I had never seen a house on fire before."

4. Read the vignette and polish it. Replace vague words and phrases with more precise expressions. Add details that complete the description, but remove anything that doesn't contribute to the picture.

5. Share the vignette with a partner. Ask the person to point out any places that could be improved.

EXTRA:
Try turning the vignette into a short story. This may involve adding characters, creating dialogue, and inventing a more exciting ending.

Model Vignette

Car Crash

I was riding in a car with my father. We had just taken a family friend to the airport, and we were on a busy street heading home for dinne. Our radio was tuned to the news station that my father always listens to. We listened to a bulletin about a bad accident that had happened in another part of town. "Glad that's not us," I said.

As we came around a curve, my father put on the brakes. At first, I didn't know why, but then I saw a car stopped down the block. Its emergency lights were flashing.

Suddenly my father yelled, "Hold on!" He was looking into the rear-view mirror. I turned and saw a sports utility vehicle approaching us fast. I knew immediately that it was going to hit us. I braced myself against the dash.

Bam. It hit. Then came a second crash as we slammed into the stalled car. I felt a sharp pain in my leg, and heard glass shattering. When our car stopped, I smelled gasoline. My father shouted, "Get out! It might catch on fire!"

I undid my seat belt, but the door on my side was bent so badly it wouldn't open. My father kicked his door open and pulled me out that way.

The big car that hit us was on the sidewalk. Ours was in the middle of the street. The stalled car that we hit was pushed far down the street by the impact. I saw a man walking toward it carrying a gasoline can. (I later learned that he owned the car and had run out of gas.)

While we waited for an ambulance I heard people saying to my father, "Gosh, you two are lucky." My father's head was cut and my leg was bleeding. I didn't exactly feel lucky, but when I saw how smashed up our car was, I understood what the bystanders meant.

I was dazed, but I remember hearing a traffic report on the radio of a car that passed by. I wondered if the news was about us. I'm sure the people going by were thinking, "Glad that's not us."

DRAMATIC WRITING BASICS

The dramatic writer creates scripts that tell performers what to say and do. Scripts also gives instructions for those who do "behind the scenes" jobs, such as directing the actors, building sets, creating sound effects, and making costumes. Most scripts contain the elements shown on the example below, which is the first page of a 12-page script.

The Three Friends

Characters
Citizen 1   Nasty
Citizen 2   Lazy
Fool   Police Officer

Act 1
It's morning in Smallville. The town's three worst troublemakers—Fool, Nasty, and Lazy—sit on a park bench near a phone booth.

(Two citizens enter from the left. Citizen 1 reads a newspaper.)

CITIZEN 1: Earthquakes. Fires. Tornadoes.

CITIZEN 2: I don't need a paper to find trouble. Our TV set just exploded.

CITIZEN 1: Trouble found me, too. My house flooded.

CITIZEN 2: My aunt broke her leg picking plums.

CITIZEN 1: Seems like trouble has moved to Smallville.

(The two citizens exit right.)

FOOL: Did you hear that? Trouble has moved to town.

NASTY: It gives me an idea. Let's capture Trouble and drive him out of town.

LAZY: Why bother?

NASTY: We'd be heroes. We might get a big reward.

The **character list** names each character.

An **act** is a section of a play that happens in one place and at one time. It is like a chapter in a book. In some scripts, acts are divided into scenes.

The **setting** tells where and when the action occurs.

A **prop** is any object used in a performance.

Dialogue consists of all the words spoken or sung by performers. Dialogue is broken into separate speeches or lines. Each speech is labeled with the name of the person delivering it.

A **stage direction** describes an action that a performer is to carry out.

EVALUATING DRAMATIC WRITING

The following points can be used for editing or judging dramatic works.

1. Does the script have a clear focus? This is important because audiences can't stop a play and think about it. To test a script's focus, see if you can sum up what it's about in one or two sentences.

2. Is there a strong beginning? Many writers feel that the main subject or problem should be introduced within the first few minutes of the performance. Often, the problem involves conflict between two characters who have different goals. What one character wants interferes with what the other character wants.

3. Does each character have a distinct personality? If two characters are similar, the audience may be confused.

4. Is each speech essential? Audiences lose interest if characters waste their breath on small talk. On the other hand, people pay attention when characters argue or reveal unexpected facts.

5. Are the props used in the performance? Objects that are handled by performers should have a real purpose. Otherwise, they may distract the audience. For example, if a character picks up a flashlight, it should be used for something dramatic.

6. Are the actions important? If the script tells an actor to open a window, that action should have a purpose in the story.

7. Does the ending make sense? Of all the parts of a drama, the ending is usually what audiences remember most clearly. For this reason, the writer needs to give extra attention to the closing moments of a script.

ONE-MINUTE PLAY

A good way to develop play-writing skills is to write short plays. The challenge is to get the audience to understand the characters and the situation within a few seconds.

DIRECTIONS:

1. Find a subject that can be dramatized in 60 seconds.
Try focusing on a short action or event, such as:
- meeting someone for the first time
- talking to someone on the telephone
- looking for something that is lost
- trying not to be seen by someone
- buying or trading something
- arguing with someone about who is next in line
- dealing with a door-to-door salesperson

2. List the characters and describe each in a few words. Short plays usually have three or fewer characters. To make sure the audience isn't confused, make the characters different from each other in an obvious way. For example, two characters might hold opposite opinions. This can lead to conflict, and that's what makes plays interesting.

3. Sum up the play's action and tone in a sentence or two. For example: "Two silly shoppers fight over a scarf while a third shopper walks off with it." A clear summary will help the author write the script.

4. Draft the script. In a one-minute play, the conflict often starts with the first or second speech. One character might immediately accuse another of doing something wrong.

5. Test the script. Read it aloud yourself. See if the lines are easy to say and if they build conflict. Then ask a partner to read the script with you while you time it. If it's too short, add material. If it's too long, cut lines.

6. Perform the script for an audience. Costumes and scenery aren't needed. Writers often present new plays by having actors read them. This is called "Readers' Theater."

EXTRA:

Videotape the play, and then share it with people who weren't able to see it "live."

Model One-Minute Play Script

Goodbye, Moon

Cast of Characters: Mad Scientist, Friend

Mad Scientist: Stand back. I'm going to push the button in 25 seconds.

Friend: Don't! If your machine works, you'll destroy one of nature's great wonders.

Mad Scientist: You think the moon is a great wonder? To me it's just ugly. 20 seconds, 19...

Friend: I'm fascinated by the way it waxes and wanes.

Mad Scientist: Same old stuff every month. 16...15...

Friend: Without the moon, there won't be any tides.

Mad Scientist: Who cares? 13...12...

Friend: Sea snails care.

Mad Scientist: I don't know anything about snails. 9...8...

Friend: Why don't you invent a way to talk to them and hear what they think about the moon?

Mad Scientist: How could I do that? 6...5....

Friend: You're a genius. You could do it. And the world would applaud you.

Mad Scientist: Really? 4...3...

Friend: Really!

Mad Scientist: 2...1...OK. I won't destroy the moon.

Friend: You'll be remembered as a hero.

Mad Scientist: Really?

Friend: At least among the sea snails.

PERSONIFIED PANEL

A panel usually consists of people who spontaneously discuss a topic in front of an audience. But with imagination a writer can create a fictional panel featuring parts of an object that come to life and talk about themselves. As the parts speak, the audience learns about the object.

I'm the mouthpiece!

DIRECTIONS:

1. Pick an object with two or more parts. Examples include an egg, a violin, a telescope, a computer, and an eye.

2. Do research to gather information about the object. It's important to understand what each part does and how the parts work together.

3. Write a few words describing the personality of each part of the thing. For example, one part might brag, another might be nervous, a third could be silly.

4. Decide who will be the moderator. The moderator could be part of the object or it could be an outsider. In either case, this character will introduce the panel and make sure all the panel members have a chance to talk.

5. Choose a tone for the discussion. Will the parts get along in a friendly way or will they argue a lot?

6. Write the script. Make sure each part gets to talk about what it does. Just as in a real panel, the parts might interrupt each other, and might get emotional.

7. Test the script. First, read it to yourself. Try using a different voice for each part. Then find a group of actors to perform the script with you for an audience.

EXTRA:

Put together a panel to discuss a subject that interests you, for example, space exploration, movies, a particular sport, or a hobby.

How to Teach Writing Without Going Crazy © 1998 Monday Morning Books, Inc.

Model Personified Panel

Parts of the Ear

Head: Welcome to our panel about how the ear works. My name is Head, and I'll be your moderator. Joining me are Outer Ear, Middle Ear, Eardrum, and Inner Ear. Together, they will explain how sound goes from the outside world into the brain. Our first speaker is the Outer Ear.

Outer Ear: Thank you, Head. I'm made of two parts. The flap, also known as the "pinna," is the part of the ear attached to the outside of the Head. It collects sound. My other part is a short tube leading to the Eardrum.

Eardrum: That's me. I'm a thin sheet of tissue. When sound waves reach me, they make me vibrate. I pass these vibrations on to the Middle Ear, who will now explain the next step.

Middle Ear: I'm an air-filled chamber and contain the three tiniest bones in the body: the hammer, the anvil, and the stirrup. The vibrations from Eardrum cause the first hammer to vibrate. This in turn causes the anvil to move, and the anvil then moves the stirrup. The stirrup sends vibrations through another membrane to the Inner Ear.

Head: Does anyone on the panel know why three bones are needed to carry sound from the Outer Ear to the Inner Ear?

Middle Ear: The three bones are made in a way that magnifies sound 20 times. Without magnification, many sounds would not reach the Inner Ear.

Inner Ear: That's me. I contain two parts. One is a set of three semicircular canals. They help the body maintain balance. The other part is the cochlea, which looks like a snail's shell and is filled with fluid. Vibrations from the oval window pass through the fluid and eventually stimulate tiny hair cells, which send electronic signals to the brain. The brain then interprets these messages as sounds.

Head: Perhaps another panel will discuss how the brain works. For now, let me thank our panel members.

RADIO PLAY

During the 1930s and 1940s, millions of people listened to radio plays. These dramas consisted of dialogue and sounds. Listeners used imagination to "see" the action.

DIRECTIONS:

1. Choose a subject. The material can be made up or based on a historic event, such as the first hot-air balloon flight. Fantasy stories work especially well because it's easy to imagine things like talking animals.

2. List the characters. Describe the personality of each one in a sentence or two. This helps when writing dialogue.

3. Outline the action. The outline should answer the following questions:
- What problem or event starts the drama?
- What scene or scenes happen in the middle of the play?
- What happens in the end?

4. Draft the script. Because listeners can't see the action, the dialogue must describe what's going on.

> **Nancy:** Look, isn't that your aunt riding a skateboard?
> **Pete:** You're right, and she's carrying her pet piranha.
> **Sound:** [Siren]
> **Nancy:** Why is that police car chasing her?

Note that sounds must be included in the script.

5. Polish the script. First, read it aloud to yourself. Use your ear to make sure the dialogue is smooth. Then have a few friends perform the parts while you listen. Make changes needed for clarity or to add drama.

6. Record the script on audiotape. When recording, have the actors sit near the microphone to avoid an echoing sound. Also, warn the actors not to rustle their scripts.

EXTRA:

Adapt familiar children's stories as radio plays, which can then be shared with younger children on tape.

Jacques, it's off the ground— the world's first hot-air balloon!

How to Teach Writing Without Going Crazy © 1998 Monday Morning Books, Inc.

The Fox and the Crow
a fable adapted from Aesop

Dog: Why are you looking up at that tree, Fox?

Fox: Shhh. Crow's up there, eating some tasty-looking cheese. I'd like a bite.

Dog: Forget it. She never shares, and you don't know how to climb a tree to take it.

Fox: But I have a plan. Watch. (calling loudly) Hi, Crow. What are you doing up there? Are you eating cheese?

Crow: Mmmmmm.

Fox: I can't understand you when you mumble.

Crow: Mmmmmm.

Fox: Of all the birds in the world, you have the most beautiful voice.

Crow: Mmmmmm.

Fox: Would you just sing a quick song for Dog and me?

Dog: She'll never do it.

Fox: (Pleading) Crow, sing a few notes, please.

Dog: (Whispering) Fox, she's opening her mouth.

Crow: (Singing) Twinkle, twink....Oh, no.

Dog: The cheese is falling.

Fox: Gulp!

Dog: You caught it on the fly.

Fox: And it was delicious.

Crow: (Calling down from the tree) That was a mean trick.

Fox: At least you learned a lesson. Don't trust flatterers.

Crow, sing a few notes, please.

She's opening her mouth, Fox!

SELF-INTERVIEW

An interview is a conversation between two people. One person, called the *interviewer*, asks questions. The other person, called the interviewee, answers the questions. In a self-interview, a writer scripts both parts.

DIRECTIONS:

1. Choose a topic that you know well. It could be an event, for example, a stay in a hospital. Or it could be a skill, for example, making model airplanes.

2. Brainstorm questions about the subject. Include short fact questions and open-ended questions:
• Short fact questions are about things like names and dates.
• Open-ended questions are usually about opinions or experiences, and seek longer responses.

3. Write a question from your list, then write the answer. Use a script form. Include your name as the interviewee, for example:

> Interviewer: How long have you been sailing?
> Sandy: For about three years.

4. If you can think of more to say, ask yourself a follow-up question. Examples of follow-up questions are: "What happened next?" and "Why did you do that?"

5. Continue asking and answering the questions on your list. Try to think up an answer that makes a good ending.

6. Test and polish the interview. Read both parts aloud by yourself. Look for places that might need a clearer answer or a follow-up question.

7. Find someone to play the part of interviewer and put on your self-interview as a short play.

EXTRA:
Use the interview format to write about a famous person. In the report, you'll write the interviewer's questions and the answers that the famous person might have given. Base the answers on library research.

How to Teach Writing Without Going Crazy © 1998 Monday Morning Books, Inc.

A Screenwriter Interviews Herself
by Julie Reynolds

Interviewer: Exactly what is a screenwriter?

Julie: Someone who writes scripts that can be made into movies.

Interviewer: Have you had a movie made from one of your scripts?

Julie: Not yet, but a movie company is working on one of them.

Interviewer: Can you tell me about it?

Julie: It's about a strange family that visits a small town. Soon everyone in town thinks that the strangers are from another planet. The townspeople don't know whether to help the strangers or try to capture them.

Interviewer: What happens in the end?

Julie: If I tell, that would spoil the movie for you.

Interviewer: How did you learn to write scripts?

Julie: I've watched many movies and have taken screenwriting classes.

Interviewer: Why do you like writing scripts?

Julie: Movies can make impossible actions seem real, for example, a flying saucer taking off. It's as if dreams or fantasies are true.

SKIT

A skit is a short, humorous play. It usually has just a few characters. Although meant to be funny, a skit can say something important about people.

DIRECTIONS:

1. Choose a subject for the skit. Skits are often about everyday activities such as: grocery shopping, getting a haircut, taking a music lesson, or waiting in line. It's also possible to write a skit about a historic event, for example, how an inventor invented something.

2. List the characters. Usually, a skit will have only two or three characters. Write a sentence describing the personality of each character. Or sketch the character.

3. Think about how to find humor in the subject. An easy way to make a situation funny is to use exaggeration. For example, in a skit about stage fright, you might decide to have a nervous speaker faint. In a skit about dealing with a telephone salesperson, the performer could come up with outlandish reasons for not buying the product.

4. Plan the beginning and the ending. For example, in a skit about someone learning to use chopsticks, the beginning might show one character urging the protagonist to eat with chopsticks. The ending might show the frustrated protagonist throwing down the chopsticks and using his or her hands to scoop up and eat the meal.

5. Draft the script. Describe the setting and props. Be sure to include stage directions, such as how a character will enter or exit the scene.

6. Test the script. First, read it aloud to yourself. Make sure the dialogue flows smoothly. Then get others to perform the parts for a trial audience. Ask for suggestions that might make it funnier. Revise the script if necessary.

7. Present the skit to a real audience.

EXTRA:
Record the script on videotape, and share it with people who enjoy watching comedy shows.

Model Skit

At the Movies

(One character—Watcher—sits in a seat waiting for a movie to start. A second character—Talker—enters, sits next to Watcher, and starts talking.)

Talker: (Loud) I can't wait for this movie to start. Have you seen it?

Watcher: (Softly) No, have you?

Talker: Ten times. I know every line by heart. You'll love it.

Watcher: We'll see. It's starting now.

Talker: The opening's great. See that guy? A giant mosquito will grab him and...

Watcher: Don't tell me. I like to be...

Talker: ...drink up all his blood. What were you saying?

Watcher: Surprised. I liked to be surprised.

Talker: Anyway, before he dies, the guy will take a ride in a flying saucer hidden in that building.

Watcher: (Sarcastically) Thanks for telling me.

Talker: Don't thank me. I like to share what I know.

Watcher: (Whispering) Shhhhh, I want to see what that girl in the red hat is up to.

Talker: Don't worry about her. She's scared at first but in the end, she saves the world. Do you want to know how?

Watcher: No. I want to see the film.

Talker: She finds this magical ring and...

(Watcher stands up and walks off.)

Talker: Hey, I thought you said you want to see the movie. Don't you want to hear what happens next?

STAGED DIALOGUE

A staged dialogue presents a conversation between two characters: one is an expert and the other is a person interested in the expert's ideas. The purpose of a dialogue is to explain the subject so that an audience can understand it.

DIRECTIONS:

1. Decide on the length of the dialogue. A dialogue that lasts for one or two minutes is a good length for a first effort. The text will fill one or two pages.

2. Choose a topic. It should be something that you understand or that you can learn about through research.

3. List interesting facts about the topic. The information should be news to the average person. For example, most people probably don't know that the invention of the helicopter can be traced back to windmills.

4. Name the characters. For example, in a dialogue about kites, the expert might be called Kite Pro. The other character could be called Announcer or Friend.

5. Draft the dialogue. Use a standard script format, in which each character's name comes before the speech:

Announcer: What's the key to flying kites?
Kite Pro: Put safety first.

To add interest, you might have the non-expert sometimes make wild guesses that are wrong.

6. Check the dialogue by reading it aloud. Make sure the information comes across in a way that is clear. If the conversation seems "slow," try shortening the speeches. Then find a partner to perform it with you.

7. Present the dialogue to a real audience.

EXTRA:

Write additional staged dialogues and record them on an audiotape. Share the tape with someone who needs something interesting to listen to when doing chores or when commuting.

What's the first rule of kite-flying?

Be safe.

Model Dialogue

The Astronomy Minute: "Seas on the Moon?"

Karen: Welcome to "The Astronomy Minute," with Sandy Blaze, the Backyard Astronomer. What's the topic today, Sandy?

Sandy: Seas on the moon.

Karen: You're kidding. The moon is dry as dust.

Sandy: True. Yet the moon has many seas, such as the Sea of Tranquility, where astronauts first landed in 1969. But of course, they didn't splash down. The Sea of Tranquility is a dry plain covered with volcanic material.

Karen: Then why is it called a sea? Was it once covered with water?

Sandy: No. But in 1609, when Galileo became the first astronomer to study the moon with a telescope, he saw large dark areas, which he thought were bodies of water.

Karen: I guess he was stupid.

Sandy: Hardly. Galileo was a genius. But his telescope was less powerful than modern binoculars. Also, since on Earth water looks dark, Galileo guessed that the moon's dark areas were water. This is called "reasoning by analogy."

Karen: But Galileo was wrong.

Sandy: That often happens in science. But one scientist's error can lead others to look for the truth. Besides, while Galileo was wrong about the seas, he was right about other things. For instance, he saw that some mountains on the moon are as tall as the Earth's tallest mountains.

Karen: I didn't know that.

Sandy: Let's talk about it on our next show.

Karen: Good idea. But for now, "The Astronomy Minute" is over.

EXPOSITORY WRITING BASICS

Expository writing is also called "informational writing." It includes many forms, such as instructions and history articles. This kind of writing can be as entertaining as fiction. However, the main goal is truth, not entertainment.

Most examples of expository writing include the following elements:

Facts: A fact is a statement usually based on an observation that can be checked. For example, if a writer says that the Eiffel Tower is 984 feet (300 m) tall, the reader could go and measure the tower to see if that measurement is correct.

Sources: In many cases expository writers do not make the observations themselves. Instead, they rely on fact sources, such as books, the Internet, or experts. To help readers decide if the facts are believable, writers will often reveal their sources. For example, suppose a news story reports that a rocket was traveling at 25,000 miles per hour (40,000 k/h). If that number came from NASA, readers are more likely to trust it than if the number came from someone viewing the rocket from a beach.

Information about the writer: Readers know that a writer's background can influence how the facts are chosen and presented. This is called the writer's "bias." One way to overcome this problem is for the writer to reveal information that might influence the way a story is reported. The writer might explain, "Although I make a living selling bicycles, I have tried to fairly (objectively) present the facts about the healthful value of bicycling." This personal information can help readers better judge the story.

Evaluating Expository Writing

The following points can be used when editing or judging expository articles.

1. Is there a clear main idea? Successful expository pieces usually focus on one important subject. If an article deals with two or more subjects, readers can become confused.

2. Is the writing clear? People who read expository writers mainly want to understand the subject. They are not interested in fancy writing. What matters most is that they can grasp main ideas, and also understand the facts. Two secrets of clear writing are:
• Use specific language.
• Make sure the sentences are not too long.

3. Are the facts interesting? Expository writing should present information that is new to the intended audience. For example, most readers won't find it interesting to read that the Eiffel Tower was built by an engineer named Eiffel. But many readers may be surprised to learn that the same man worked on the Statue of Liberty.

4. Are the sources of the information identified? When unusual facts are given, readers won't know where they came from. This way, they can check on the accuracy of the facts if they want to.

5. Are facts distinguished from opinions? Opinions can add interest to a piece of expository writing, but it is important that opinions are not presented as facts.

6. Is the reader helped to understand how the facts fit together? Because readers can get lost in facts, the careful writer will lead the reader from point to point, much as a museum guide will take visitors through a museum, explaining the meaning of the entire exhibit, and also each part in it.

DIAGRAM

A diagram is a drawing that explains how a thing works by outlining its parts. It often includes words that discuss each part of the diagram.

DIRECTIONS:

1. Choose an object that has several parts. It should be something that can be studied firsthand. Examples include: a can opener, eyeglasses, a flashlight, a hole punch, a musical instrument, scissors, and a tennis racket.

2. Research the subject for background information. For example, if you don't know the names of the parts, ask an expert, or look in a special kind of reference book called a visual dictionary or visual glossary. Libraries often have one or more of these books.

3. Draw the object. Although you could copy a drawing from a book, you will understand the object better if you make an original drawing.

4. Write a short introduction. You might give the history of the object, plus other interesting facts, for example, unusual ways it's used.

5. Add labels for each part. The label should name the part and explain how it works and/or what it does.

6. If you used reference books to collect facts for the labels, add a source list. For each book, include the title, the author, the publisher, the date, and the page.

7. Test the diagram. Show it to someone who doesn't know much about the object. Ask the person if there is anything about the diagram that needs further explanation. Then revise the diagram.

8. Share the diagram. You might post it on a bulletin board or send it to someone who is interested in the object.

EXTRA:
Do the same activity with a complicated object, such as the eye or a jet engine. Base the diagram on research gathered from an expert or from reference books.

The Safety Pin

A better name for the safety pin might be the "spring pin." This is because the coil works as a spring to push the two shafts apart.

Early safety pins were used in Greece more than 2,000 years ago. The modern form of the device was patented in 1849 by Walter Hunt, who sold the rights to his patent for a few hundred dollars.

Coil: The coil acts as a spring.

Shafts: These two "sides" of the pin are pushed apart by the tension in the coil.

Point: The point makes it possible to pierce materials that are to be pinned.

Head: The head serves as a clasp that locks the material together. The head also serves as a guard to protect users from being stuck by the pointed end of the pin.

Head: The head serves as a clasp that locks the material together. The head also serves as a guard to protect users from being stuck by the pointed end of the pin.

Point: The point makes it possible to pierce materials that are to be pinned.

Coil: The coil acts as a spring.

Shafts: These two "sides" of the pin are pushed apart by the tension in the coil.

Sources
Eggplants, Elevators, Etc.: An Uncommon History of Common Things by James Meyers (Hart, 1978), pages 236 - 238.

What's What: A visual glossary of everyday objects—from paper clips to passengers ships, edited by Reginald Bragonier, Jr. and David Fisher (Ballantine, 1981), page 204.

FAQs

People often have the same questions when they encounter something new, such as a school they've just entered or a piece of computer software. Instead of waiting to answer each person's question when it's asked, an expert may prepare a list of these "Frequently Asked Questions" along with their answers. This kind of list is called an FAQ.

DIRECTIONS:

1. Choose a topic. It should be something that you know a lot about either from first-hand experience or from research. FAQs can be written about hobbies, pets, sports, tourist attractions, scientific phenomenon, historical events, buildings, movies, and so on.

2. List about five important questions about the topic. These should be questions that people who haven't studied the topic might ask.

3. Write the answers to the questions. Be concise. Focus on the most important ideas.

4. Decide what order to use in presenting the questions and answers. Alphabetical order is often used.

5. Polish the text. Try to read each answer from the point of view of someone who doesn't know much about the topic. Look for places that need clarification. In some cases you might want to add an illustration or diagram to make the explanation clearer.

6. Share your FAQ with someone for whom the material will be new. Ask this trial reader to point out places that are puzzling. Revise the text as needed.

EXTRA:
Write an FAQ about modern life that would answer questions of someone from the distant past.

How to Teach Writing Without Going Crazy © 1998 Monday Morning Books, Inc.

Model FAQ

Palo Alto FAQs

Many important computer and high-tech companies began in Palo Alto, California, including Hewlett-Packard, Apple Computer, and Sun Microsystems. If you're new to Palo Alto, here are the answers to questions you might have.

Attractions: What are interesting things to see in town?
<u>Answer</u>: Stanford University should be at the top of your list. Stanford is one of the leading centers of higher education in the world. The 10,000 - acre campus includes a famous shopping center and an 18 - hole golf course.

Also visit Foothills Park, which provides views of San Francisco Bay and, on clear days, San Francisco itself, which is 30 miles (48 kilometers) to the north.

Baylands Park is a nature preserve on San Francisco Bay, where you'll see many species of birds while watching small planes land and depart from the airport.

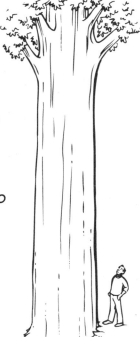

Cultural facilities: What does the town offer in terms of the arts and education?
<u>Answer</u>: For a small town, Palo Alto has many cultural services. The Lucy Stern Theater complex features theater productions for adults and kids. Nearby is a small science museum, a children's library, and the main library.

Name of the town: Where did Palo Alto get its name?
<u>Answer</u>: "Palo Alto" is a Spanish phrase. The Spanish word *Palo* means "tree." *Alto* means "tall." When Spanish explorers first came to this area, they camped near a very tall redwood tree. Later, the town was named for that tree.

Population: How many people live in Palo Alto?
<u>Answer</u>: The population is about 50,000.

HOW-IT-WORKS ARTICLE

A how-it-works article explains a process, for example, how the stomach digests food. This kind of writing is often used in science and technology.

DIRECTIONS:

1. Choose an object that performs a function. It can be natural or manmade. Examples include the ear, a bird's wing, a faucet, and a lock.

2. If you don't know how the thing works, do research. Gather information on the following subtopics:
• what each part of the object does
• what materials are used, for example, film in a camera
• how the parts work together to carry out the process

3. Draft the article. It may include the following:
• a title that describes the subject
• an introduction that explains what the object does and gives background information
• steps that show each part or phase of the process
• one or more diagrams if needed to make the process clear

4. Share the article with an expert. Ask the person for suggestions that would make the article more accurate. Then revise the article.

5. Test the article. Ask a few readers who know nothing about the process to read the article and then explain in their own words how the thing works. You might also ask them the following questions:
• Is the article clear?
• Is the information interesting?

6. Share the article. You might try to get it published in the school or local newspaper, or send it to someone who would be interested in the subject.

EXTRA:
Turn the how-it-works article into a presentation done in front of an audience or done on videotape.

Opening and Closing a Twist Faucet

Have you ever twisted the handle of a faucet and wondered how it works? Here's your chance to find out.

Turning on the water

1. The faucet handle is rotated, usually in a counterclockwise direction. The handle acts like a lever to increase the turning force, known as torque.

2. The handle turns a grooved faucet stem, at the end of which is a washer that acts as a plug.

3. As the stem turns, it screws out of the cylinder. This pulls the washer out of the stem seat, and unplugs a hole in the faucet body.

4. Water then flows through the faucet and out the spout.

Turning off the water

5. The handle is rotated in the opposite direction.

6. This turns the stem, which moves back into the cylinder.

7. The pressure from the cylinder squeezes the flexible washer into the valve seat. Although the water in the pipe and faucet body is under great pressure, the grooves in the stem keep it from being pushed out.

8. If the washer is worn out and unable to make a tight seal, some water will slip between the washer and the valve seat. In this case, the faucet will drip or allow water to flow.

HYPOTHESIS

A hypothesis is an intelligent guess about how something works or why it happens. For example, suppose you wonder, "Why is an egg oval-shaped and not round?" After thinking awhile, you might guess that a round egg could roll out of a nest and break. That hypothesis might be the starting point for research to discover the facts of the matter.

DIRECTIONS:

1. Think up a question whose answer you don't know. Some examples are:

- How does a vacuum cleaner pick up dirt?
- Why do we dream?
- Why do electrical plugs have more than one prong?
- Why do people have fingerprints?
- Why can't we see stars during the day?
- Why does glass break?
- Why are there silent letters, for example, the *g* in *sign*.
- Why do people get a fever when they're sick?
- Why does a piano have 88 keys?

2. Try to answer the question based on your background knowledge. For example, suppose you don't know why ice floats. You might think about other things that float, for example, wood. Can you find ways that ice and wood are alike and that might explain why they float?

3. Write an essay about the hypothesis. An essay is a short, nonfiction composition. Your hypothesis essay might:

- Describe the subject.
- State the question.
- Describe the guess (hypothesis) that might be the answer.
- Explain what led you to that guess.

4. Test your hypothesis with a trial reader. See if the person agrees with your hypothesis or has other ideas that might make more sense. If you like, revise your essay.

EXTRA:
Do research to find out if the hypothesis is supported by facts.

Remembering Facts

People carry around a lot of information in their heads. This information includes dates, names of people, scientific facts, so on.

For example, if you ask me for my address, I can immediately give it to you: 1111 Greenwood Avenue. Or if I want to call a friend on the telephone, and if I know that person's phone number, I can think of it in an instant.

The question is: how do we find one fact among the thousands or millions of other facts that we have learned?

One possibility is that the brain stores information the way a library stores nonfiction books. In the library, nonfiction books are grouped by subject. The math books are in one place; the sports books are in another. Each group has a general number, and each book in the group has its own specific number that's like a street address. Once you know that number, you can quickly go to the book.

Maybe the brain places all the facts we know into categories, and then stores them in different places in the brain. Here's an example. If someone asks me, "How many planets are there?", maybe the word "planets" points to the place where my brain stores information about planets. The words "how many?" might point to a section in the planets area containing number information.

INSTRUCTIONS

Writing instructions is a form of teaching. The goal is to teach readers how to do an activity or learn a skill. Often, a set of instructions will also include interesting background information.

DIRECTIONS:

1. Choose an activity that you're good at. It could be a game like chess, an activity like juggling, a school skill like solving math problems, or a hobby like making model airplanes. It should be something that you could teach to readers in a page or two.

2. If the activity is complicated, choose just a part of it. For example, if flying model airplanes is too big a subject, you could focus on just one part of it, for example, landing a plane.

3. Do the activity or review it in your memory. Take notes on each important step. List materials that are needed.

4. Draft the instructions. You might do the following:
• Give the piece a descriptive title.
• Write an introduction that tells why it is worth learning.
• Give the directions for carrying out each important step. If a step is too long, try breaking it into two steps. Include warnings about anything that might cause a problem.

5. Create illustrations if needed. Sometimes a drawing or a diagram can clarify a difficult part of the activity.

6. Test the directions. Ask a trial reader to point out places that are confusing or that need additional information.

7. Polish the instructions. Try them yourself as a final check.

8. Share the directions. You might give them to someone who would like to try the activity.

EXTRA:
Make a book of useful instructions on a single topic or on a variety of topics.

Model Instructions

How to Give a Speech with Confidence

Do you tremble at the thought of speaking before a group? If so, you're not alone. Many people fear public speaking. But you don't have to live with this problem. The following suggestions will help you become comfortable when giving a speech. You might even learn to like it.

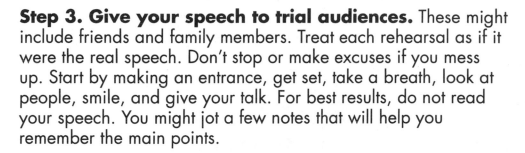

Step 1. Know what you want to say before you stand up. Trying to figure out your presentation at the time you're giving it is a big mistake. Some people are good at improvising. But if you're not one of them, write out your speech ahead of time.

Step 2. Rehearse by yourself. Practice the speech on different days until you know it. This doesn't mean memorizing the words, but getting to know them really well so that the delivery is natural.

Step 3. Give your speech to trial audiences. These might include friends and family members. Treat each rehearsal as if it were the real speech. Don't stop or make excuses if you mess up. Start by making an entrance, get set, take a breath, look at people, smile, and give your talk. For best results, do not read your speech. You might jot a few notes that will help you remember the main points.

Step 4. If you will give the real speech in a place that is new to you, visit it ahead of time. Walk around. Get a feel for the room. This way, it won't seem strange to you.

Step 5. During the actual presentation, make eye contact with some people. In every group, you can find a few listeners who will be rooting for you to do well. Their smiles and nods will give you energy and encouragement.

Step 6. Afterward, think about your presentation. Give yourself credit for strong points, and figure out ways to improve areas that didn't go as well as you wanted.

ORAL HISTORY ARTICLE

One way to learn about a time in the past is to interview someone who lived then.

DIRECTIONS:

1. Find someone who has memories of a time that interests you. This could be a relative or a neighbor.

2. Make an appointment with the person. Explain that you want to find out about the past. Tell the person how much time you will need for the interview. Often an hour is plenty of time.

3. During the meeting, ask the person to describe the incident or period. Don't interrupt, but if you have a question, ask it during a pause. As the person talks, write the words. Skip every other line to make it easier to read your notes later on. (Some historians prefer to use a tape recorder and then write the notes later.)

4. After the meeting, edit the material. Omit words and phrases that aren't needed, for example, "ums" and "ers." Write a short introduction that tells something about the person who is sharing the memories about the past. When reviewing your work, think about the following points:
• Is it clear?
• Does it include interesting facts and details?
• Does it have a clear beginning and ending?

5. Go over the article with the person who told you the history. Correct mistakes and add missing information. You might ask the person to loan you photographs if that will help make the story clearer.

6. Share the history. You might send it to someone who is interested in the period you researched, or see if a local newspaper will publish it.

EXTRA:
Imagine someone in the future interviewing you about an event in your life. Try to imagine what that person would want to know about changes that you've seen. Write an oral history of the event as if you were looking back on it.

Model Oral History Article

My neighbor, Eric Haas, was born in 1942. Here is his account, in his words, of how television entered his life.

Our First Television

I was about nine years old when we got our first television. I'm not sure of the year. I think it was 1951.

Before we got our television, the Lakes, who lived across the street, got a set. The screen was round and about the size of a salad plate. We used to look out our window at the Lakes' TV. Their set was so small, we could hardly see anything except a glow. My brother and I used binoculars to see what was on, until our mom caught us and said it was bad to stare into someone else's house.

A few months later we got our own set. It arrived in a big truck. Two men carried it into our house. The set itself was a huge piece of furniture, but the screen was tiny. Of course the picture was in black and white.

I remember the first show I watched was *The Lone Ranger*. Everyone watched it. Kids who didn't have sets went to the homes of friends who did. The theme song was the William Tell Overture, and it became so popular, we bought a record of it. The records, by the way, were large disks that spun at 78 rpms (revolutions per minute). A record played for only three minutes.

Eventually, our family began to eat dinner in front of the set, using metal trays on stands. It almost didn't matter what was playing. We were fascinated by it.

Those early sets would often break. Then, a repairman would come to our house to fix it. Usually, this involved putting a new tube into the set. TV repairmen were very important in those days because if the TV went out, everyone would get very unhappy. Sets were so expensive, few people could afford to go out and buy a new one.

I think it took about two years before we got used to having a television and thought of it as something ordinary. Nothing as exciting as that happened again for a long time, until the invention of the personal computer.

RESEARCH PAPER

A research paper is a report that focuses on a question, such as "How do ants walk?" The writer finds and presents facts that answer the question. The facts can come from many sources, such as books, articles, videos, and Web sites.

DIRECTIONS:

1. Choose a subject. A research paper can be about almost anything, including space, games, people, and things.

2. Brainstorm questions about the subject. For example, if the subject is pigs, questions might include "Do pigs make good pets?" and "Are pigs really dirty?"
Choose one question. This will be your research topic.

3. Collect facts that help answer the question.
• Write each fact and its source on a separate note card. This makes it easier to organize the facts later.
• Don't copy the facts. Instead, paraphrase them. By putting ideas into your own words, you'll understand them better.
• If a fact seems strange, find a second source to check it.

4. Organize the information. You can make an outline that puts the points in order. Or draw boxes, and then fill them in with your main points.

5. Draft your report. You might do the following:
• Give it a specific title.
• In the introduction state the topic.
• In the main part present the facts clearly and concisely.
• Include notes that give the source of each fact. Do this by placing a number after the fact. The information can appear at the bottom of the page or on a separate page.
• Add drawings or other illustrations if needed.

6. Test the report with a trial reader. See if the person understands the paper. Make changes based on the reader's comments. Check all spelling and punctuation.

7. Share the report. You might do this orally, or you might have it published in the school newspaper.

EXTRA:
Send a copy of the report to someone who is interested in the topic.

Model Research Paper

The Easy-to-Play Woodwind

Although made of brass and not wood, the saxophone is actually classified as a woodwind instrument. Other woodwinds include the oboe and the clarinet.[1] Of these three instruments, the saxophone is considered the easiest to play.[2]

To play notes on a clarinet or on an oboe, the musician uses fingers to cover holes in the instrument's body. The fingers must cover the holes precisely in order for the notes to be properly sounded. It's different with the saxophone. To play notes on this instrument, the saxophonist presses padded keys. The pads fit snugly over holes in the instrument's body. The musician does not have to accurately cover the openings.[3]

Of course, when Antoine Sax invented the saxophone in the 1840s, he wasn't trying to make an instrument that was easy to play. He was simply interested in creating a new sound. At the time, he thought that the saxophone would be used in marching bands that were becoming popular.[4] He had no idea that the saxophone would eventually become an important instrument in jazz, a form of music that originated in New Orleans and became popular after Sax died.[5]

Notes

1. *The Concise Columbia Encyclopedia* (Avon, 1983, p. 924).

2. Conversation with Fred Schwartz, music teacher.

3. Personal experience of the author.

4. *Word People* by Nancy Sorel (American Heritage, 1970, p. 253).

5. *Listening to America* by Stuart Flexner (Simon and Schuster, 1982, p. 85).

SPEECH INTRODUCTION

Someday you may be asked to introduce someone who will make a speech. When you do an introduction, your job is to prepare the audience to listen to the main speaker.

DIRECTIONS:

1. Gather information from the speaker. This might include:
• The person's name, including how to pronounce it
• Interesting facts about the speaker's background, including the person's education, work, honors, and experiences
• The title of the speech
• The main points that the speech will cover
• The goal of the speech
• Whether or not the speaker will answer questions

2. Draft the introduction. Keep it short. You might:
• Give a hint about the subject.
• Mention the speaker's name in the first few sentences.
• Encourage the audience to "welcome the speaker," which is a signal for them to applaud.

3. Test your introduction. Read it aloud first to yourself and then to a trial audience. Make sure it flows smoothly. Time it to make sure that it isn't too long.

4. If possible, show the introduction to the speaker a day or more ahead of time. Ask the person to check the facts and to suggest any additions.

EXTRA:

Pick a famous person from history. Study that person's life, and then write an introduction to a speech that the person might give.

How to Teach Writing Without Going Crazy © 1998 Monday Morning Books, Inc.

Model Introduction to a Speech

Introduction to
Dr. Beverly Calvin's speech entitled
"Amazing Fleas"

Many people think that fleas are disgusting. I own a cat and a dog, and have had some bad experiences with fleas. If you've ever been bitten by a flea, you know what I'm talking about.

However, today's speaker, Dr. Beverly Calvin, looks at fleas differently. She is an entomologist, a scientist who studies insects. She has spent the past 20 years studying fleas. Her research has taken her to more than two dozen countries around the world.

In her speech today, which is titled "Amazing Fleas," Dr. Calvin will share many incredible facts. For example, did you know that there are nearly 2,000 different kinds of fleas?

You may wonder why anyone would want to study fleas. The answer is that these tiny insects are responsible for a great deal of disease. By studying them, scientists try to find ways of solving the problem.

Dr. Calvin also says that fleas are fascinating. For example, a flea can jump more than 100 times its own height. If a person could do that, it would be like jumping higher than a skyscraper.

Dr. Calvin has written many scientific articles on fleas. But she also enjoys helping non-scientists understand these insects. And I'm sure we'll enjoy listening to her. She hopes you'll be more interested in fleas when she's finished talking, even if you still think they're horrible.

Now let's welcome Dr. Beverly Calvin.

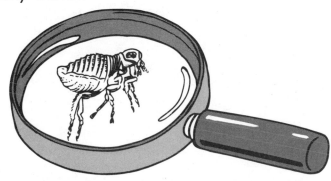

WEB SITE LISTING

A Web site is a collection of information on the Internet. Some Web sites feature unusual and valuable information. Others have little value. By describing a Web site in detail, you can help people find sites that are worth visiting.

DIRECTIONS:

1. Look for sites that interest you. Although sites are often mentioned in newspapers and books, the way to find sites is to use a search device such as Yahoo.

2. Before writing a review of a site, take notes. Write down the following kinds of information:
- the name of the site, for example, "The Constellations and Their Stars"
- the site's URL (Internet address), for example:
        http://astro.wisc.edu/~dolan/constellations
- the name of the person or group who created the site
- the purpose of the site
- the major topic or topics found there
- the media used, such as text, photos, drawings, maps, sounds, animations, interactive experiences, and videos
- the organization of the material
- the kinds of links that connect the site to other sites
- the most recent update

3. Form an overall opinion of the site. Do you think it's good, bad, or average?

4. Write the listing. In the first paragraph tell what you think of the site. Give specifics to back up your judgment. If you have visited other sites that deal with the same topic, you might compare the various sites. End with a rating.

5. Test your listing by sharing it with a trial reader. Ask the person if the writing is clear. Make corrections that are needed.

6. Share your listing. You might do this on paper, for example, in an article for the school newspaper. Or you might send it as e-mail to friends who are online.

EXTRA:
Write a series of Web site listings on a topic, for example, "The Best Sites About Camels."

Model Web Site Listing

The Constellations and Their Stars
http://www.astro.wisc.edu/~dolan/constellations

If you are interested in star gazing, "The Constellations and Their Stars" may interest you. This fact-rich site offers clear and fascinating information about 88 constellations, from Andromeda to Vulpecula. Because all the constellations are covered, this resource will be equally valuable to readers in the northern and southern hemispheres.

There's a lot of material here, including many diagrams and pictures. However, you won't get lost because everything is presented in a logical order.

The Web master is Chris Dolan, a doctoral student in astronomy at the University of Wisconsin. Dolan says that he enjoys helping teachers and students, and he includes his e-mail address so that people can write to him. However, he warns that he will not be fooled into writing reports for anyone, saying, "I have received some hilarious e-mail from kids trying to avoid doing their homework."

Besides covering the constellations, the site features information and links on related topics such as:
• the 26 brightest stars and the 26 nearest stars
• the moon phases
• planetary positions
• backyard astronomy
There's even an article warning against wasting money trying to pay to have a star named for you or someone you know.

The site is continually being developed. It was updated just a few weeks before this review was written.

"The Constellations and their Stars" was visited more than two million times during a recent three-year period. Popular sites are not always worthwhile, but this one is.

Overall rating: On a scale of 1 (low) to 10 (high) this site earns a score of 9.0.

"WHAT IF?" ESSAY

"What if people never had to sleep?" Or "What if animals could talk?" Trying to answer such questions requires imagination. This kind of thinking and writing can lead to new ideas in science, art, and daily life.

DIRECTIONS:

1. Pick a topic. You can write speculative essays about anything, for example:
- Historical events: What if Columbus had failed to reach land?
- Future events: "What if we enter a new Ice Age?"
- Nature: "What if insects could communicate with us?"

2. Write several "what if" questions about your topic. Then choose the one that interests you the most.

3. Brainstorm possible answers to the question. These will often take the form of results. For example, if you asked, "What if scientists cure the common cold and the flu?", results might include:
- never needing to carry tissue or a handkerchief
- never needing to get a flu shot
- not worrying about people sneezing on you

4. Draft your essay.
- Start by thinking up a descriptive title.
- Write an introduction that presents the "what if" question.
- Use your notes to write the body of the essay.
- Think up a real ending, for example, the most unusual result on your list.

5. Test your essay with a trial reader. Ask for suggestions that would make it more interesting, for example, by adding even more surprising results. Change the essay if you can improve it.

6. Share the essay. Send it to someone you know who has an interest in imagining the future.

EXTRA:
Turn your essay into a story that presents the ideas through characters, plot, conflict, and so on.

Model "What if?" Essay

What If Everyone Could Read Minds?

Sometimes I feel that people can read my mind. For example, my brother sometimes says something to me at exactly the same time I am thinking it even though we have not been talking about that subject.

I know that he can't really read my mind, because I have tested him thinking certain thoughts, for example, "If you can read my mind right now, say so." It never happens.

But what if we all had ESP? What if I could know exactly what you were thinking, and you could know exactly what I was thinking, and we both could know exactly what everyone else was thinking? The world would be different.

For example, no one would lie. A lie wouldn't fool people because everyone would know what the liar was really thinking. So people would be totally honest, whether they wanted to be or not.

Also, there would be no more surprise parties. How could anyone surprise you if you knew they were thinking about surprising you?

Politics would also have to change. Politicians often make promises that they know they can't keep. But if everyone had ESP, no one would believe a false promise.

Sports would change, too. For example, in baseball, a batter would know what pitch a pitcher was planning to throw. Maybe baseball players would have to stop thinking. The same would be true in chess and other strategy games.

At school, there wouldn't be any tests with fact questions like "What's the world's longest river?" You'd know the answer by reading the mind of the smartest classmate, or the mind of your teacher. Only tests of skills would make sense, for example, writing an essay like this one.

NARRATIVE BASICS

Narrative writing is also called story writing or fiction. It takes many forms, such as the novel and the fable. Most stories include the following elements.

Characters are the people or animals appearing in a story. A character can also be something that acts like a person, for example, a robot.

Plot is what happens in a story. Usually there will be one main action, for example, a hunt for a treasure.

Setting includes when and where a story happens. Some stories have many settings.

Dialogue is what characters say. These words are usually placed inside quotation marks, for example, "Run!"

Narration is the description of each setting, action, and character.

Theme is the lesson that the story teaches, for example, "Telling the truth is better than lying."

Evaluating Narratives

The following points can be used when editing or judging stories.

1. Is there a clear central action? Examples are: a race, an escape, a fight, or a hunt for something.

2. Are the characters interesting? Readers are drawn to characters who take on a tough job, for example, rescuing a friend. Most stories include several kinds of characters:
• Protagonist (hero): Readers root for this character.
• Antagonist (villain): This character causes problems for the protagonist and other characters. Villains often add excitement to a story.
• Victim: The protagonist tries to help this character.
• Fool: This character gets into trouble on his or her own.

3. Is the setting an important part of the story? Writers often do research to find details for describing settings, especially those located far away or long ago.

4. Is the plot well made? Most plots include:
• A "trigger event" that upsets the protagonist's life.
• Scenes of conflict between the protagonist and the antagonist. The reader wonders, "Who will win?"
• A scene called the "climax" in which readers learn who wins.
• A final scene called the "anticlimax" that tells the reader what happened to all the main characters.

5. Is the narration clear? If a character describes the action, this is called a "first person" story. If the author describes the action, it's a third person story.

6. Is the dialogue important? Most authors avoid small talk such as "Hi" or "See you later." Instead, they want the dialogue to add interest to the story, for example, by describing the action: "Look, the boat is on fire!"

7. Does the story have a powerful theme (lesson)? Sometimes, as with fables, the theme is stated in the story. More often, readers must discover the theme on their own.

FABLE

A fable is a story that teaches a lesson about how to behave. Most of the characters are animals who talk and think like people, but keep some of their animal characteristics. For example, a bird may talk but also fly.

DIRECTIONS:

1. Make a list of behaviors. Most fables deal with negative conduct such as:

- gossiping
- being selfish
- lying
- bullying
- being lazy
- bragging
- being a pest
- playing mean jokes on people

2. Pick one behavior as the subject of the fable.

3. Choose an animal that will display the behavior. If possible, the animal's real behavior or physical qualities should relate to the action you chose. For example, if your subject is gossiping, you might pick a squirrel because when squirrels chatter, it may seem as if they're gossiping.

4. Think up one or more other characters for the story. These might be other animals or people. In many fables, two characters will be different in an important way. For example, one will be fast (the hare) and the other will be slow (the tortoise).

5. Write a story about the behavior. For example, a butterfly might spend so much time showing off its beautiful wings that it doesn't notice a butterfly collector who's about to capture it. As with other kinds of stories, fables usually include suspense or drama, so that the reader at first isn't sure what will happen.

6. Add a moral. This is a sentence that sums up the lesson of the story in the form of advice, for example, "Don't pretend to be something you are not."

7. Share the fable with a trial reader. Ask for suggestions that might make the lesson more powerful or the story more dramatic. Then edit the story as needed.

EXTRA:
Turn the fable into a radio play or a skit.

Model Fable

The Loudest Mosquito

Two hungry mosquitoes entered a house in search of their dinner. As they approached a sleeping victim, one mosquito buzzed loudly.

The other mosquito said, "Shhh. You'll wake him."

The noisy mosquito responded, "You're just envious because I can buzz louder than you and any other mosquito around here. In fact, I'm probably the loudest mosquito in the whole world."

The quiet mosquito shook its head. "You're wrong. I just don't want any trouble."

But the first mosquito buzzed even louder. "I'm not just the loudest mosquito in the world. I'm the loudest mosquito who ever lived!"

Indeed, the mosquito's buzzing almost shook the house. Suddenly, the person who was sleeping woke up and clapped his hands together. The noisy mosquito was flattened.

Now the room was very quiet, except for the other mosquito who quickly flew out the window.

Moral: Bragging can lead to its own punishment.

GROUP STORY

Most stories are written by one or two authors. But sometimes one writer will arrange for a team of coauthors to work on a story. Each coauthor adds a paragraph. The result can be filled with twists and turns that surprise even the person who started the tale.

DIRECTIONS:

1. Write a letter to your coauthors that describes your project. The letter might tell how many people will take part and what the story's tone will be, for example, humorous or scary. You might include rules such as:
- Write between 25 and 50 words.
- Use description and dialogue.
- End your section with a line that gives the next writer a hint about what might happen next, for example:
    A strange noise came from the box. What could it be?
- Complete your part within one day.
- Return the story to me when you're done.

2. Write a working title and the first section. This opening should introduce the protagonist and the setting.

3. Give the letter and the opening to the second writer.

4. Continue this way until each writer has had a turn.

5. Write the final section. This should tie together all the loose ends.

6. Share the story with all the coauthors. Later, you might make copies for others to read and perhaps continue the story.

EXTRA:
Publish the group story in the school newspaper or literary magazine, or on the school Web site if there is one.

How to Teach Writing Without Going Crazy © 1998 Monday Morning Books, Inc.

Model Group Story

The Trained Monkey

Writer 1. The plan was so simple. The idea had come to Henrik while he was watching a TV commercial in which a monkey scrambled eggs. Henrik thought, "If a monkey can be trained to do that, why not train it to do something useful?"

Writer 2. By useful, Henrik meant training a monkey to do his job, which was folding fliers for an advertising company. Henrik arrived at the office each night after the other workers had gone. It was a boring job, but it wouldn't bore a monkey. Henrik would be free to do what he liked best, sleep. So he used his savings to buy a monkey.

Writer 3. As you know, some monkeys are well-behaved and others just like to have fun. The monkey that Henrik bought was full of mischief.

Writer 4. Not knowing which kind of monkey he had, Henrik took the monkey to work with him. On the first night the monkey seemed interested when Henrik showed him how to fold the fliers.

Writer 5. On the second night, Henrik watched as the monkey folded each flier. Henrik chuckled to himself, "I'll be able to nap every night."

Writer 6. The third night, Henrik trusted the monkey to fold the fliers by himself. Henrik set his watch alarm, curled up in a ball, and went to sleep under the desk. "I have nothing to worry about," Henrik mumbled.

Writer 7. When Henrik awoke, he stood up and rubbed his eyes. He couldn't believe what he saw! The monkey had folded every flier into a paper airplane. The office was littered with the flying fliers. What was Henrik going to do?

Writer 8. With only one hour until the rest of the office workers arrived, Henrik quickly taught the monkey how to unfold the airplanes, smooth out the fliers, and refold them correctly. Together, they got the job done. After that, Henrik decided it was better for him to do his job himself.

Writer 1. Henrik kept the monkey, anyway. On weekends, they went to the park and sailed paper airplanes together.

HISTORICAL FICTION

Historical fiction starts with a real event from the past. It differs from regular historical writing because it includes scenes and dialogue that are not based on fact, but which might have happened. Usually, it includes historical characters and characters made up by the writer.

DIRECTIONS:

1. Choose a historical subject. This could be an event, for example, the building of a famous bridge. Or it could be a well-known figure, for example, an explorer, an inventor, or a soldier.

2. Research the subject. Successful historical fiction must be woven around facts. For example, a fictional story about Leif Ericsson might tell when he lived, where he lived, what kind of boat he built, and who sailed with him.

3. Create one or more fictional characters who will interact with the historical figures. For example, a story about Leif Ericsson's travels might include a made-up sailor who was on Ericsson's boat.

4. Write the story. Use all the regular devices of storytelling: action, dialogue, and so on. The ending might involve something that actually happened in the past.

5. Share the story with a trial reader. Ask if the historical setting seems real. Then edit the story as needed.

EXTRA:

Write a story in which a real person from the past gets to visit the present. For example, what would happen if Queen Elizabeth I came to your town?

How to Teach Writing Without Going Crazy © 1998 Monday Morning Books, Inc.

Model Historical Fiction

Touching Words

Many people say that Paris is the world's most beautiful city. I don't know even though I've lived here all my life. That's because I'm blind. But many years ago, I witnessed a great historical event.

In 1819, I was living at the Institute for Blind Children. In those old days, many blind children became beggars. The Institute was one of the few places where blind children got any real education. But even there, we had only three books in the library. These books used raised letters, and were difficult to read.

Then a boy named Louis Braille came to live at the Institute. He had lost his sight in an accident. But he told me, "I'm lucky. My father believed that I could learn and insisted that I attend our village school. Now he's sent me here to get even more education."

Louis and I often talked about current events. Our favorite topic was Napoleon, who had recently lost the battle of Waterloo and was exiled on the island of St. Helena. We frequently analyzed the general's strategies.

Unknown to us at this time, a soldier named Charles Barbier had invented a code for sending messages at night using raised dots and dashes. Barbier thought that his code could help blind people, and he brought it to the Institute. The system was complex. I told Louis, "This is worse than trying to read a book with those raised letters."

Louis said, "It's just a start. It can be improved so that blind people can read as well as everyone else."

"Who's going to improve it?" I asked.

"I will," said Louis. That was the beginning. He spent weeks experimenting. There were many failures. Then finally he created a simple system. It used combinations of six dots to represent all the letters of the alphabet, plus punctuation marks, numbers, and arithmetical signs.

Blind students who tried Louis's plan loved it. Louis adapted his method to musical notation, and became admired for his organ concerts.

Unfortunately, government officials preferred the old system. They tried to block Louis's invention, and it wasn't until after Louis's death that the world came to appreciate his great gift, which they named in his honor.

RECYCLED COMIC

Although pictures are important in comics, the words spoken by the characters are equally important for telling the story. By changing the words, a new comic story can be created.

DIRECTIONS:

1. Find a comic strip. It should include several dialogue balloons in which characters talk.

2. Paste or tape blank paper over the dialogue balloons. Also, cover any description in the narration boxes.

3. Study the pictures. On scratch paper, draft new dialogue that will tell a different story using the same pictures.

4. Use pencil to carefully letter the new dialogue into the blank balloons. If there are narration boxes, write in new descriptions.

5. Share the comic with a trial reader. Ask for suggestions that might make the story clearer and the dialogue more interesting. If you like, use the feedback to edit the text.

6. Go over the words with ink. Then gently erase the penciled lettering.

EXTRA:
Use the same method to transform an entire comic book story.

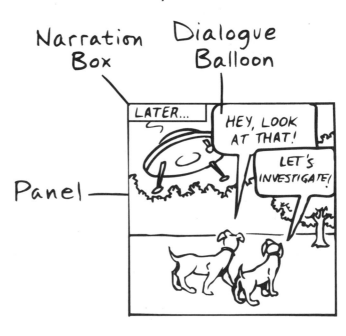

Model Recycled Comic

Original Version

New Version

RETOLD STORY

Many well-known writers have created new stories based on old ones. For example, the movie *King Kong* is a retelling of an old fairy tale, "Beauty and the Beast."

DIRECTIONS:

1. Choose a story to retell. Pick one that your readers will be familiar with.

2. Decide how to change the story.
Some possibilities are:
• Updating the story. This means changing the setting from the past to the present or even the future.
• Flipping the story. This means changing an important detail. For example, you can make the hero into the villain and the villain into the hero.
• Expanding the story. This means adding details and events, but not changing the main points in the plot.
• Changing the tone. This means turning a dramatic or serious story into a comedy, or turning a comedy into a serious story.
• Changing the form. An example would be turning a prose story into a poem, or turning a play into a short story.

3. Draft the story. You might give it a new title and also rename the characters.

4. Test the story. Share it with a trial audience. Ask for suggestions for improving the story. This might involve adding a scene or making the dialogue more interesting.

5. Polish the story. Give careful attention to the descriptions. Check the dialogue by reading it aloud. Include a note that names the original story and the author if known.

EXTRA:
Write a story from scratch. Then experiment with it by retelling it in a way that includes an important change. For example, you might turn the hero into the villain, and the villain into the hero.

Model Retold Story

The Three Bicyclists and the Bully

Once upon a time—actually, it was last Thursday afternoon—I was bicycling to the park to fly a kite with my brother and sister. "I'll get there before you two," I shouted, and zoomed ahead of them.

As I approached the park, a big bully jumped out from behind a tree and blocked my way. "Give me that bicycle," he growled. "I want it."

He was about a head taller than me, and twice as heavy. His fists looked like hammers. I told the bully, "Sure, you can have this old bicycle if you really want it. But my brother is coming along, and he's got a much newer, shinier bike. Why not wait and take his?"

The bully looked at my almost-new bicycle, and then asked, "Is your brother's bicycle really better than yours?"

"Judge for yourself," I answered. "Here he comes."

The bully let me go ahead.

I pedaled on a short way, and then stopped to see what would happen. As my brother approached the tree, the bully jumped out again. My brother's taller than me, but not quite as tall as the bully.

"Give me that bike," ordered the bully.

"This piece of junk?" asked my brother. "Take it if you like. But then you'll miss out on a really fabulous bicycle that'll arrive here any second."

"Is it better than yours?" asked the bully.

My brother nodded, and the bully pointed for him to go on.

Then up rode my sister. Again, the bully leaped out and yelled, "Give me that bicycle." But my sister never even slowed down. She just rode right into the bully.

He yelled at her, "I'll get you."

I wish he had tried. My sister has a black belt in karate. But the bully will to have wait until another day to learn what that means because the wind was blowing and we wanted to launch our kite.

Note: This story is based on "The Three Billy Goats Gruff." The author is unknown but the story was first published by Hans Christian Anderson.

SEQUEL

The word *sequel* means "to follow." A sequel is a story that follows or grows out of an earlier story. It usually involves the same characters who take part in a new adventure.

DIRECTIONS:

1. Choose a well-known story. It could be a short story, a fable, a legend, a novel, or even a movie.

2. List the main characters.

3. Think up a new plot for the characters. Try to imagine what might happen if the same characters got together again after the original story ended.

4. Write the story. It's all right to add new characters or change some of the behaviors of the old ones. The goal is to invent a new story based on the old one. For example, if the old story told about a trip to an enchanted village, the new story might describe a trip to a different type of place.

EXTRA:

Write a prequel. A prequel is a story that comes before another story, but has many or all of the same characters. For example, a prequel to *The Wizard of Oz* might tell about Dorothy's life in Kansas before the storm carried her to Oz.

How to Teach Writing Without Going Crazy © 1998 Monday Morning Books, Inc.

Model Sequel

The Three Bears Visit Goldilocks

"Look at this mess," said Mama Bear, as she walked through the house.

Papa Bear frowned. "It'll cost a fortune to replace the furniture."

"We ought to go and make her pay for this," suggested Baby Bear.

"Excellent idea," said Mama Bear.

That afternoon, the bears walked to Goldilocks' house. They knocked, but no one answered. Baby Bear turned the knob. The door opened.

"Should we go in?" he asked.

"Since she entered our place without permission, there's no reason we can't enter hers," said Mama Bear, stepping into the house.

On the dining room table, they found a sandwich, a bowl of soup, and a soda. After taking a bite of the sandwich, Papa Bear spit it out and grumbled, "Yuck, it has mayonnaise on it. I hate mayonnaise."

Mama Bear sipped the soup and then made a face. "Too salty." She pushed the dish onto the floor.

Baby Bear tried the soda and said, "It's just right."

Next, the bears went to Goldilocks' room. Papa Bear started playing with a pogo stick but he was too heavy and bent it. Mama Bear got onto Goldilocks' skateboard and crashed into a CD player. Wanting to avoid trouble, Baby Bear just used the cell phone to call a friend who lived on the other side of the world.

At this point, Goldilocks came home and yelled at the bears. "I'm phoning the police and having you arrested."

"Go ahead," said Baby Bear. "After we tell the police what you did to our house, you'll go to jail for twice as long as us."

Goldilocks thought about this, and then nodded her head. "You're right," she said. "Besides, I started it by entering your house without permission. I'm really sorry."

"We're responsible, too," said Mama Bear. "Just because you made a mistake didn't meant that we should do the same thing."

The bears helped Goldilocks clean up the mess. Later on, Goldilocks went to the bears' home and helped fix their things. This led to a friendship that lasted many years.

TALL TALE

A tall tale is a funny story or description based on exaggeration.
For example:

> Yesterday was the coldest day in history. It
> was so cold that our thermometer insisted on
> wearing mittens. Even the ice was shivering. In fact,
> it was so cold, our furnace refused to turn on, and
> instead stayed in bed. We turned on the radio to
> get the weather news, but it was so cold, the radio
> waves froze in mid-air and we didn't hear them until
> there was a warm spell.

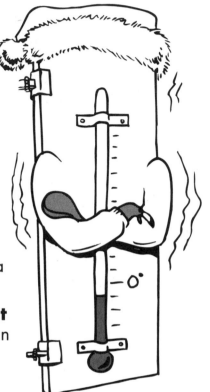

DIRECTIONS:

1. Choose a subject. It could be a person, a place,
or an event.

**2. Write a sentence that exaggerates something
about your subject.** With a person or pet, you might use a
word such as *tallest, smartest,* or *friendliest.*

**3. Brainstorm a series of examples that prove what
you said about your subject.** Each example should be an
exaggeration that is so outrageous, no one will believe it but
everyone will laugh because of it.

**4. String the examples together to describe one or
more incidents or an entire story.** As you string together
the exaggerations, try to make each one "bigger" than the one
before it.

5. Share your tall tale with a trial reader. See if the
person laughs at the right places. Ask for suggestions that might
make the material even more outlandish.

6. Try drawing an illustration to go with the tale. The
illustration should be as exaggerated as the words.

EXTRA:

Make a book of tall tales. Write all the tales yourself, or collect
tales written by other authors.

Tall Tale Starters

Tall tales can be about anything. Pick a topic on this list and start a tale—"I have the world's messiest closet—or think up your own ideas.

Closet: neatest, messiest

Computer game: most difficult, most exciting, most realistic

Dream: scariest, silliest

Friend: most faithful, stubbornest

Gift: worst

Haircut: best, worst

Luck: best, worst

Manners: best, worst, strangest

Mosquito: most annoying, hardest to catch

Movie: most boring, scariest

Pet: dumbest, smartest, most loyal

Picture: prettiest, ugliest

Robot: smartest, strongest

Roller coaster: scariest, tallest

Test: most difficult

Villain: scariest

Weather: strangest, wettest, windiest

Weekend: most boring, most exciting

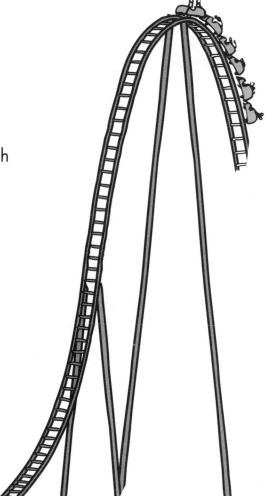

PERSUASIVE WRITING BASICS

Persuasive writing aims to convince readers to accept an opinion. Sometimes it also tries to get readers to do something, for example, to contribute to a charity. This type of writing takes many forms, including campaign speeches and advertisements. Most examples include:

• **The opinion that the writer wishes to "sell."** This will usually be expressed in a sentence that states the idea that the writer believes to be true. An example would be: "Space exploration is an important activity."

• **Arguments that support the main opinion.** These will include facts, other opinions, and examples. Usually, it takes more than one argument to change a reader's mind.

• **An attack against the opposite opinion.** For example, to convince readers that basketball is the best sport, a writer might tell what's bad about other sports.

• **Repetition.** Many readers don't understand or pay attention to an idea the first time they hear it. For this reason, writers may restate the arguments. However, because repetition can be boring, writers will usually try to hide it by using different words. Repetition is often used in advertising.

• **Appeals to the heart.** Persuasive writers know that people often change their minds if they feel happy or angry about a subject. That's why persuasive writers often include humor or emotional language in their writing.

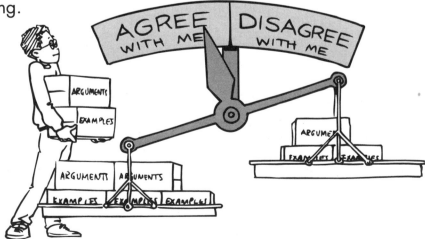

How to Teach Writing Without Going Crazy © 1998 Monday Morning Books, Inc.

Evaluating Persuasive Writing

The following points can be used when editing or judging writing that is meant to persuade readers.

1. Is the opinion clear? Can you tell what the writer wants readers to think or do? Clear opinions usually can be summed up in a single sentence, for example:
- Eat more vegetables.
- Go see this movie.
- Vote for Candidate X.
- Always be on time.

2. Does the writer effectively support the opinion? Are there enough reasons? Is each reason convincing?

3. Does the writer deal with arguments that could be made against the opinion? Showing the weaknesses in the opposing arguments is a good strategy.

4. If repetition is used, is it done in a way that is interesting? For example, are different words and phrases used?

5. Does the writer seem to care? Emotion by itself is not an argument. But if a writer can show genuine feelings about an issue, this can attract the attention of readers. One way that writers show feelings is by revealing something about themselves. For example, when urging readers to exercise, a writer might explain how exercise made a difference for a friend.

BOOK REVIEW

A book review does more than describe a book's contents. It tells readers whether or not the book is worth reading.

DIRECTIONS:

1. Choose a book to review. Reviewers write about every kind of book, including novels, how-to-do-it guides, biographies, poetry, and children's books.

2. Take notes while reading the book. Start with the title, the author, the publisher, and the publication date.
• If it's nonfiction, list the contents.
• If it's fiction, describe the main characters and the plot. Also, look for a short passage that you could quote in the review as a way of showing the writer's style.

3. Form an opinion. Is the book good, bad, or mixed?

4. Draft the review. Reviews often contain these parts:
• Introduction: This gives the book's title, author, and subject. It may include the reviewer's opinion of the book.
• Description of contents: If the book is fiction, this will be a plot summary. If the book is nonfiction, this will list the main topics covered by the book.
• Excerpt: This is a short passage showing the author's style.
• Comparison: The reviewer tells how the book is like or different from other similar books by the same author or other authors.
• Recommendation: The reviewer tells who, if anyone, might enjoy reading the book.

5. Share the review with a trial reader. Ask for suggestions that would make the review clearer or more interesting.

6. Publish the review. You might have it printed in a school newspaper or send it as a letter to a pen pal.

EXTRA:
Use the same format for writing a movie or TV program review.

Model Book Review

Albert Payson Terhune's *Lad: a Dog* is one of the best animal books ever. Dog lovers will love it. Cat lovers will love it. Even people who don't like pets will love it.

Although the book reads like a novel, it's actually a collection of twelve stories. These tales trace the life of Lad, a real collie. Lad lived on a country estate in New Jersey during the first part of the twentieth century.

In the book, the collie has many amazing adventures. These include capturing a burglar, killing a rattlesnake that's about to attack a child, and saving a woman who fell into an icy lake.

Terhune claimed that the stories were totally true, but that's hard to believe. For one thing, several stories describe what happened to the dog when no human was around, for example, when Lad is lost in New York City:

> At a rivulet, a mile beyond, he stopped
> to drink. And he drank for ten minutes. Then he
> went on. Unmuzzled and with his thirst slaked,
> he forgot his pain, his fatigue, his muddy and
> blood-caked coat, and the memory of his
> nightmare day. He was going home.

Readers may also have trouble believing the story when Terhune describes the dog's thoughts and feelings:

> Yes, he was lost. And he realized
> it—realized it as fully as would a city dweller
> snatched up by magic and set down amid the
> trackless Himalayas. He was lost. And Horror
> bit deep into his soul.

Although parts of the book are hard to believe, the writing and the action make it worth reading.

COMPLAINT LETTER

A complaint letter tells a business or organization about a problem and suggests a way to solve it.

DIRECTIONS:

1. Outline the points you want to make. A complaint letter usually does the following:
- Tells who the writer is
- Describes the problem
- Proposes a solution and explains why this idea makes sense
- Gives a deadline for action

2. Draft the letter. Write each point concisely and clearly. Use a tone that is calm and business-like.

3. Review the text. Consider the words from the point of view of the reader who will get the letter. Add details that will improve the chances of getting the desired results. Remove any material that might upset the other person.

4. Write the final version using the business letter form. Many business letters are done in block style. This means that there is a blank line between paragraphs. Be sure to include your return address and the date.

5. Send the letter. If the person deals with your complaint in a satisfactory way, be sure to send a thank-you note. If the person does not respond favorably, write another letter.

EXTRA:
Write a complimentary business letter. For example, if someone gives especially good service, write a letter to the person's boss describing the employee's action.

Model Complaint Letter

1111 Green Avenue
Palo Alto, CA 94301
May 27, 1998

Bracken's Family Grocery Store
Village Shopping Center
Palo Alto, CA 94302

Dear Mr. Bracken:

My family has shopped in your grocery store for five years. We have spent thousands of dollars there, and have also recommended the store to our neighbors.

Unfortunately, I had a bad experience a week ago. I purchased a box of your store brand raisins, but when I opened it at home, I found a dead insect inside. The next day, I returned to the store to get a new box of raisins.

I spoke to a clerk named Jerry, who said he could not give me a new box without seeing the old one with the insect. I told him I had thrown it away. (The bug was disgusting!)

Jerry said he thought it was impossible for an insect to be in a sealed box. I asked him if this meant he thought I was lying. He said he didn't care what I was doing, but that he would not give me a new box.

If you want to keep me as a customer, you will have to do the following within a week: One, give me a new box of raisins. Two, apologize for the way Jerry handled the problem.

Sincerely,

Lance Denker

LETTER TO THE EDITOR

The letters column of a newspaper or magazine gives readers a chance to share information and opinions. Although the letters are addressed to the editor, they are really directed to everyone who reads the publication.

DIRECTIONS:

1. Choose a topic to write about. Most letters to the editor are about articles in the publication or about a letter from another reader. The best letters usually involve a strong opinion.

2. Summarize the main point in a single sentence. Doing so will help you write a letter that is clear and strong.

3. Draft the letter. When drafting the letter, you might:
• Summarize the article or topic your letter will deal with.
• Tell about yourself and why the topic matters to you.
• Give your opinion about the topic, and information that might interest other readers.
• Outline an action that readers can take to support your ideas. An example would be asking readers to contribute to a cause or to write a letter to a government official.

4. Test the letter. Ask a trial reader for suggestions that might make the letter clearer or more powerful.

5. Polish the letter and then mail it. Most publications require that you include your home phone number.

EXTRA:

Read the publication to see if your letter is printed. Then keep reading in case someone responds to what you wrote. You might then write a follow-up letter responding to what the other person wrote.

How to Teach Writing Without Going Crazy © 1998 Monday Morning Books, Inc.

Model Letter to the Editor

To the Editor

Your editorial (April 18) argued against lowering the voting age. This is an insult to young people like me. Worse, it damages our society because it prohibits many smart people from helping guide our government.

You wrote that young people don't have enough real life experience to take part in politics. Maybe you've never met any young people, but we do live in the real world and we have many important experiences. Young people have to deal with traffic when we bike-ride. We make money decisions when we shop. We read books all day long. Many of us even have jobs, either at home or in the community. (I started working in my parents' clothing store when I was eight!)

In school from the earliest grades, we learn about government. I believe most students think more about how government works than the average adult. We not only read and write reports on the subject, we also take part in school elections.

In my opinion, the best way to decide who should vote would be to give a test about how government works. The test could also deal with common sense and logic. Anyone who can pass the test should be allowed to vote. Even a ten-year-old? My answer is "Yes" if the ten-year-old can pass the test. Don't forget that when he was three, Amadeus Mozart was writing wonderful music. Age doesn't matter!

I hope that all those who agree with me will write to their representatives asking them to get rid of the age requirement for voting.

Irwin Hill

OPINION ESSAY

When you write an opinion essay, you try to prove that something you believe is really true.

DIRECTIONS:

1. Brainstorm several opinions that you hold. These might be about things that you think are the best, for example, best writer, sport, food, or season. Opinions can also be about the future, for example, whether or not time travel will be possible some day.

2. Choose one opinion and state it in a clear sentence. For example, "Cats make better pets than dogs" or "Dogs make better pets than cats."

3. Brainstorm arguments supporting your opinion. You might list the benefits of owning a dog, for example, a dog provides companionship and protection.

4. Brainstorm arguments <u>against</u> the opinion, and then answer those arguments. For example, some people say they don't want to own dogs because they'd have to walk them. You might answer that argument by pointing out that walking a dog is good exercise for people.

5. Draft the essay. This may include:
- a descriptive title, such as "Six Reasons to Own a Dog"
- an introduction that identifies the opinion
- arguments for the opinion and against the opposite
- a conclusion that sums up the arguments or that gives the strongest reason supporting the opinion

6. Review the essay. Ask yourself how someone who believes the opposite might feel about it. You might also get a reaction from a trial reader. Make any changes that strengthen the case for your opinion.

7. Share the essay. You might try to publish it in a newspaper or send it to a friend.

EXTRA:
Write an editorial for your school paper. An editorial is a persuasive essay that usually ends by urging readers to take a certain action.

Model Opinion Essay

Watching TV Is a Waste of Time

Some things on TV are probably worth watching. However, most programs are worthless. They don't give you anything to think about or to remember. Instead, they put you into a kind of daze, except for the commercials which wake you up enough to sell you a product you don't need.

You might think it's all right to be in a daze. You might think it's relaxing. True, but that's what we have sleep for. Every night you have about eight hours to sleep and dream. You really don't need more than that.

If you agree with me, you might wonder what you'll do with all your free time if you stop watching TV. There are all sorts of interesting activities that might interest you. They're just not shown on TV, so I'll list a few to start you thinking.

Instead of being glued to the set, you could be learning a musical instrument, improving a sport skill, working on a job, building a telescope, inventing a new product, or just having fun with friends.

For example, if you spent an hour a day practicing drawing, in a year or two you would have a skill that would give you a lot of pleasure. You might even be able to make money drawing pictures for people. Or if you spent an hour a day kicking a soccer ball, you might end up as a star.

There isn't enough paper in the world to contain all the interesting skills you could develop if you had the time. You would have the time if you didn't throw it away watching television.

POETRY BASICS

Stained-glass windows have two purposes. First, they tell a story or describe something. Second, they invite viewers to notice the glass itself—its color, shapes, and texture. Poems work the same way. They communicate stories and ideas. At the same time, they call attention to language. Here is a sample poem—a limerick—and a few of the methods poets use to put the focus on words.

There once was a dog who meowed.

He often performed for a crowd.

His voice was as fine

As a friendly feline,

And even his mother was proud.

- **Writing in lines instead of sentences**

- **Rhyming**

- **Creating rhythmical "beats"**

- **Using alliteration** (bringing together words that start with the same consonant)

- **Using onomatopoeia—words that imitate natural sounds**

- **Making unexpected comparisons**

Meow.

Evaluating Poetry

The following points can be used for evaluating poetry. Because there are many kinds of poems—haiku, sonnets, limericks, song lyrics, and so on—no one poem needs to use every technique.

1. Does the poem bring attention to language?
Successful poems often contain lines that are easy to remember.

2. Is the wording fresh? Poets are always looking for new ways to express familiar ideas. For this reason, they usually avoid rhymes and phrases that are already well known.

3. Does the poem appeal to the senses? Most poems are meant to be heard. A good way to understand and appreciate a poem is to read it or listen to someone else read it.

4. Does the poem mean anything? In addition to putting a spotlight on language, poems should describe their subjects or tell stories.

"The time has come," the Walrus said,
"To talk of many things:
Of shoes,—and ships—and sealing wax—
Of cabbages—and kings."

FOUND POEM

Poets work line by line. A good way to practice this kind of writing is to break an ordinary prose passage into lines. The result is called a "found poem." It won't rhyme, but it will have the rhythm of poetry.

DIRECTIONS:

1. Choose a short passage to rewrite. It could come from a newspaper, a magazine, a letter, an advertisement, or any other piece of prose. You may need to read several articles before finding one that will work.

2. Break the passage into lines. Each line should contain a thought or a description. Usually, a line will not be an entire sentence. You may need to experiment to see where to make the best breaks. Hint: Read the lines aloud and let your ear guide you.

3. Omit material that is not needed. For example, you can remove a sentence or even part of a sentence if it doesn't fit the flow.

4. Repeat a line if you want to emphasize what it says. However, do not add new material. Everything in a found poem should be found within the original material.

5. Test your poem by reading it aloud to a trial audience. Ask for suggestions that might make the poem read in a smoother, more meaningful way.

Hey, get your poetry!

6. Polish the poem. In the finished version, include a brief introduction that gives the source of the original material. Include the name of the author if available.

EXTRA:
Make a display that shows the original material side by side with the found poem.

Model Found Poem

The article in the box comes from the *San Francisco Chronicle* The article was translated into a poem by breaking sentences into lines. Part of one sentence was deleted, and one sentence was repeated.

> ### Pacifica's Planting Sunshine
> by Mark Simon
>
> In storm-battered Pacifica, a group of residents is going to plant the seeds of spring on Monday.
> Led by Mark Stechbart, a member of the Chamber of Commerce board of directors, the group is going to scatter eight pounds of California poppy seeds on median strips and hillsides along Highway 1 and at public places all over town.
> Within a couple of months, the seeds will yield blooms of yellow, gold and orange that will drench Pacifica in the colors of the sun.

The Seeds of Spring

In storm-battered Pacifica
A group of residents
Is going to plant
The seeds of spring
On Monday.

The group is going to scatter
Eight pounds of California poppy seeds
On median strips
And hillsides
Along Highway 1
And at public places
All over town.

Within a couple of months
The seeds will yield
Blooms of yellow, gold and orange
That will drench Pacifica
In the colors of the sun.
In the colors of the sun.

NARRATIVE POEM

A narrative poem tells a story in rhyme. Like other story forms, it includes characters, dialogue, setting, plot, and a narrator. This type of poem is sometimes called a ballad.

DIRECTIONS:

1. Choose a subject. A rhymed story can be about anything. Examples include a baseball game ("Casey at the Bat"), the arrival of a guest ("A Visit from St. Nick"), and a meeting with a mysterious bird ("The Raven").

2. Plan the story. You don't need a detailed outline, but you should know the key points:
- the setting
- the trigger event that begins the plot
- the main action or actions
- the ending

3. Decide on the rhyme pattern. In some poems, the first and second lines rhyme, then the third and fourth, and so on. Here's an example from "Casey at the Bat."

> The outlook wasn't brilliant for the Mudville nine that day:
> The score stood four to two, with but one inning more to play.

4. Brainstorm rhyming words that fit your subject. For example, if you're writing a rhyming story about a magical kite, you might list rhyming pairs such as:
- kite: bright, fright, might, night, right, sight
- tail: fail, gale, hail, sail, snail, trail, wail
- twine: line, mine, pine, sign

5. Draft the poem. Keep the lines similar in length. Because rhyming while telling a story isn't easy, leave room between lines to make changes. If you get stuck, rearrange word order so that a line ends with a different word.

6. Test the poem by reading it aloud. Look for ways to make the rhymes more interesting. Add, delete, or change words to make the rhythm smoother.

7. Share the poem. Read it aloud to an audience.

EXTRA:

Tape record the poem and send it to someone who enjoys listening to poetry.

How to Teach Writing Without Going Crazy © 1998 Monday Morning Books, Inc.

Model Narrative Poem

The Test

I dreamt a dream! What can it mean?
The chalkboard was erased and clean,
And my teacher, with a smile,
Passes the quizzes down the aisle.

And I said, "A quiz today?"
Instead of studying, I had played.
My teacher shook his head and said,
"It's chapter six, you should have read."

I looked around at all my peers,
Then swallowed hard to calm my fears.
The test was numbered one to nine.
And then the bell rang. No more time!

But what was this? It couldn't be.
The bell was my alarm, oh, gee.
The test a dream, all in my head.
And I was home in my own bed!

RHYMING PICTURE BOOK

Small children love rhymes. That's why many children's writers use rhyming poetry to tell stories and teach lessons.

DIRECTIONS:

1. Choose a subject that will interest little kids. A children's book can tell a new story or retell an old one. Or it can teach about nature, everyday objects, and people.

2. Plan the book. Will it have a separate poem on each page, or will there be one long poem that continues through the book? Also, will there be a picture on each page?

3. Draft the text. Think about words that little children will understand.

4. Test the rhymes by reading them aloud. Be ready to rewrite the lines many times to make them read smoothly. If you find a line that is hard to read, try to improve it by changing a word or two.

5. Prepare the art. Most children's books are illustrated with drawings. But some use photographs, collages, holes cut in the pages, and even pop-up devices.

6. Prepare the pages. Think about the following:
• Type of paper used for the front and back covers
• Whether or not the text and art will be printed on both sides of the paper
• Kind and size of the lettering

7. Bind the finished book. There are many ways to make a book. These include: stapling, using brass fasteners, and sewing with yarn. Another option is to use a special binding machine, often available at photocopy stores.

8. Share the book. You might do this by reading it aloud to a single child or presenting it to a group.

EXTRA:
Make additional copies of the book and give them as gifts.

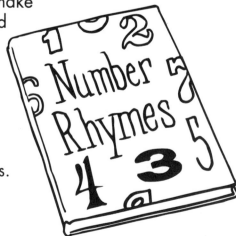

Model Pages from a Rhyming Picture Book

The first number
is the number one;
There's just one moon
and just one sun.

On each foot
you wear a shoe;
One plus one makes
the number two.

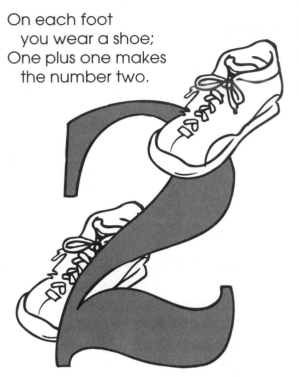

How many eggs
do you see?;
Let's count them now:
one, two, three.

If the bird lays
just one egg more;
The number of eggs
will then be four.

SONG LYRICS

Most songs consist of a melody and lyrics (the words). The person who writes the words is called the lyricist.

DIRECTIONS:

1. Borrow an old tune or write an original melody.

2. Pick a topic. Songs can be written on just about any topic, such as airplanes, sports, planets, holidays, money, hats, grammar, famous people, cities, and friendship.

3. List the main idea of the song. For example, a song about Mars might focus on going to live there. The title could be "Moving to Mars."

4. List the ideas the song might cover. For example:
• Mars is red.
• Mars is mysterious.
• We're going to Mars some day.
• There's no air on Mars.
• Many stories have been written about Martians.
• Mars is the fourth planet from the sun.

5. Draft the lyrics. As you work, keep the melody in your mind by singing or humming it.

6. Test the song. First, sing it to yourself. If you hear rough spots, edit the words. Later, sing the song to someone else and ask for ideas to improve it.

7. When printing the lyrics, include the music or name the tune. This way, other people will be able to sing the song.

EXTRA:
Record the song on tape, accompanied by a piano, a guitar, or a band. If you are using a tune by a known musician, you may need to get permission to use the melody when performing for an audience that has paid to hear the music.

Kangaroos, Elephants, Manatees, and Whales

(to the tune of "Jingle Bells")

Kangaroos, elephants, manatees, and whales,
Angelfish and llamas, ostriches and snails.
They have one thing in common, now guess it if you can.
They all share planet Earth with an animal called man.

So let's all lend a hand,
And keep this planet safe.
We want to share our land
With each animal and race.

Now, take a look around,
And hold each other's hand.
Isn't that a pretty sound?
Peace rings across the land!

Oh, kangaroos, elephants, manatees, and whales.
Angelfish and llamas, ostriches and snails.
They have one thing in common, now guess it if you can.
They all share planet Earth with an animal called man.

PARAGRAPHING

- -

There is one reason for paragraphing. When we break a long text into smaller chunks—either by indenting or by inserting blank lines—the material is easier to read and understand.

The only "rule" that most writers follow is that in a story, a paragraph should begin with each change of speaker. Other than that, paragraphing is largely a matter of taste and "feel." When tested, experienced writers often break identical passages differently. Fortunately, the location of a paragraph break is less crucial for readability than that the material is indeed divided into eye-pleasing chunks.

The following activities can help students become more aware of paragraphing, and more interested in it.

Counting Paragraphs: Have students estimate the number of paragraphs in an article, and then count the paragraphs.

Summing Up Paragraphs: Give students a passage containing half a dozen or more paragraphs. Have them sum up the content of each paragraph in a sentence.

Paragraphing Text: Retype a story or article as an undivided block of material, and number each line. Give students the handout, and have them use the paragraph mark (¶) to indicate where paragraphs should start. Have students discuss their choices in groups, then review the text.

Writing One-paragraph Essays: Suggest a topic (mirrors, mud, bicycling, pets, music) and have students discuss it in a single paragraph. All the sentences should relate to the subject. Students can share their paragraphs in small groups or on the board. For more structure, specify the purpose of the paragraph, for example, to state an opinion:

> I see people everywhere looking at themselves in mirrors as if seeing something important. If you are one of these mirror watchers, break the habit. There are many amazing things in the world, but you won't see them if you waste your time admiring yourself.

Note: Not all paragraphs have topic sentences. Sometimes the paragraph's concept is revealed only by reading all of its sentences.

- -

Hunting Paragraphs: Describe various forms of paragraphs, and have students find examples in their reading. For example:

- *Main idea followed by examples or reasons*:

    I'd never like to visit the moon. For one thing, it's hot enough during the day to boil water. At night it's way below freezing. Even worse, there's no air, so you have to wear a bulky spacesuit whenever you walk outside.

- *Chronology of an event*:

    I woke late today. I dressed in thirty seconds. When I reached the kitchen, I realized immediately there was no time to eat breakfast. I grabbed my books and dashed outside, but I was too late. The bus was pulling away.

- *Comparing and Contrasting*:

    In some ways, the hand and the foot are similar. Both have five appendages and flat areas. However, there are also differences. You can make a fist with a hand, but not with a foot. Also, you can form a circle with a thumb and another finger, but you can't using your toes.

- *Question and Answer*:

    What's so important about space exploration? For one thing, it reminds us that humans have a lot in common. For another, we expand all sorts of technical and scientific knowledge using instruments such as the Hubble Telescope. Even more important, in my opinion, we remind ourselves that exploration is an important part about being human.

Creating Paragraph Types: Have students, first in pairs and then solo, create examples of each type of paragraph.

Adding a Sentence: Write a paragraph on the board. Then ask students to think up a sentence that could be added to it, at the beginning, in the middle, or at the end.

Writing Essays with a Set Number of Paragraphs: It could be a three-paragraph theme, a five-paragraph theme, whatever. The number is arbitrary. But specifying some number will motivate students to think about paragraphing.

PROOFREADERS' MARKS

Capitalize. $\underline{\underline{}}$

<u>australia</u> = Australia

Use lower case. /

I l̸augh. = I laugh.

Delete text.

I d̸o see = I see.

Insert text. ∧

jmp = jump

Insert a punctuation mark.

It works = It works. ⊙

Insert a space. #

Wak̸eup = Wake up.

Move together. ‿

un til = until

Move text to a new location.

I sad am. = I am sad.

Begin a paragraph. ¶

This is a ⱡDemonstration of how proof reading marks are⌄used. The text in the top⌄box is a rough draft that contains many mistakes and has been marked up by a proofreader the same material appears in the bottom box after it has been corrected! Can you see that using proofreading marks is a quick way to show how a manuscript should be revised? Try using them in ⊙own your writing.

This is a demonstration of how proofreading marks are used. The text in the top box is a rough draft that contains many mistakes and has been marked up by a proofreader. The same material appears in the bottom box after it has been corrected.

Can you see that using proofreading marks is a quick way to show how a manuscript should be revised? Try using them in your own writing.

ROOTS and PREFIXES

Root	Sample words
aster	asteroid, disaster
bio	biography, biology
cap	capital, captain, caption
chron	chronicle, chronometer
dict	dictator, dictionary
dyna	dynamo, dynamic
geo	geography, geology
graph	graphic, telegraph
ject	eject, inject, reject
legis	legal, legislate
manu	manual, manufacture
mis/mit	missile, mission, admit
mot	motion, motor
ped	pedal, pedestrian
pel	propel, repel
philo	philosophy
phono	phonics, telephone
port	import, portable,
rupt	disrupt, erupt
script	description, inscription
sect	bisect, dissect
sign	design, signal
tele	telemetry, television
thermo	thermometer, thermostat
tract	traction, tractor
viv	revive, vivid

Prefix	Sample words
ab-	absent
ad-	admire
auto-	automatic
bi-	bicycle
centi-	centimeter
co-	cooperate
com-	complain
de-	defrost
dis-	disobey
ex-	except
extra-	extrasensory
hydro-	hydroelectric
il-	illegal
im-	impossible
mis-	mistake
non-	nonsense
pre-	preheat
pro-	propel
re-	return
semi-	semicircle
sub-	subtract
super-	supermarket
sym-	symphony
trans-	transform
tri-	triangle
un-	untie
uni-	uniform

VOCABULARY BUILDING

Building a strong vocabulary does not require genius. Most students can become word savvy by trying easy—and entertaining—activities.

Reading: Quantity is important, but so is variety.
• Content: Students should read about many topics, including those that they know little about. You might challenge them to read a book in each of the library's major nonfiction categories.
• Form: Students should read all sorts of writing, such as poetry, drama, journalism, and fiction.

Word-in-the-News Reports: Have each student search a newspaper for an unfamiliar word, then write a mini-report that includes the word's definition, the sentence it was found in, and a phonetic spelling. Share the reports orally or on a Words-in-the-News Bulletin Board. For example:

> <u>Word</u>: *concurring*
> <u>Definition</u>: agreeing
> <u>Phonetic spelling</u>: kon kur ring
> <u>Sentence</u>: The judge wrote a concurring opinion.
> <u>Source</u>: San Francisco Chronicle, February 1, 1998

Original Definitions: Teach the steps for writing a definition:
1. Give a general category that the word fits in:
> *chair*, a piece of <u>furniture</u>
2. Add information that distinguishes the word from other words in the category:
> *chair*, a piece of furniture <u>used for sitting by one person, and consisting of four legs, a seat, and a back rest</u>

Now ask students to define words without using a dictionary. Include words that refer to concrete things (bus, computer, shoe), and words that refer to abstractions (anger, fear, joy, justice, equality). In addition to the definition, students should use each word in a sentence.

This is a good partner activity. After the definitions are written, students might share them on the board and discuss them. Another follow-up is for students to compare their definitions with those found in a dictionary.

- -

Etymology Reports: Have students present brief word histories. For example, "Month comes from an ancient word for *moon*. A month was the amount of time it took for the moon to go through a complete cycle of waxing and waning." Research for these reports can be done using general dictionaries or etymology references.

Word Family Reports: Divide the class into small groups, and have each group report on a word family, for example, the "ped" family, which contains *pedestrian*, *pedestal*, *impede*, *podiatrist*, and *pedal*. Have the students explain the meaning of the root, and then teach important words in that root's family. (See page 121 for a list of roots.) Use the same approach to develop awareness of prefixes, such as anti, il-, ex-, proto-, re-, and tele-. (See page 121 for a list of prefixes.)

Translations: Ask students to rewrite short passages in their own words. The goal is to use as few words from the original as possible. For translation starters use material from newspapers, magazines, poems, novels, your literature text, or wise savings. For example: the saying "If at first you don't succeed, try, try again" might be translated into:

> Suppose you fail to reach a goal. Instead of quitting, make another effort. If that doesn't work, keep at it.

Word Comparisons: Ask students to explain how pairs of words are alike and different. For example: *buy/shop*:

> *buy/shop*: To buy means to pay for something and become its owner. To shop means to look for something to buy. You can shop and not buy something, but if you buy something, you own it.

Product Names: Choose a generic product and have students create new names for it. For example, a flashlight might be named: Handlight, Portobeam, or Carrylight.

Children's Nonfiction Books: Have students choose a topic they are studying—the rain cycle, photosynthesis, cosmic dust, whatever—and try to explain it in terms a first grader might grasp. This will, of course, require very careful word choice and selection of examples.

WRITERS' GROUP GUIDELINES

When you take part in a writers' group, you get to test your writing with a friendly audience. Seeing how people react to your writing can give you ideas about improving your work. You also get to help other writers.

WHEN SHARING YOUR OWN WRITING...

1. Decide what to read. Usually, it's best to share just a page or two. If you have a longer piece, select a section.

2. Tell the group what the project is about. For example, you might say, "This is a science fiction story about bees who can talk." You might ask listeners to focus on a specific area, such as the beginning.

3. Share the work. You can make copies for each person to read silently. Or you can read your work aloud while group members listen. Even if you're reading aloud, you might want to hand out copies so others can follow along.

4. Ask for comments. Listen to what people say. Take notes if you like. If someone points out a problem, don't argue. Try to understand what the person is saying. Remember, everything that is said is just a suggestion. You get to decide whether to accept it or not. During the meeting, simply thank each person who makes a comment.

WHEN HELPING ANOTHER WRITER...

1. If you have a copy of the work, read it carefully. If it's OK with the writer, make notes on the manuscript. Otherwise, use your own paper. If the writer reads the work aloud, listen carefully and don't interrupt.

2. Start with a positive comment. Writers need to hear what's good as well as what needs work. Be specific. For example, you might say,"The ending was a big surprise."

3. Be specific about parts that may need more work. Instead of saying, "Your beginning is bad," try to explain what's wrong, for example, "I think the second paragraph can be dropped because it repeats the first one."

4. If something puzzles you, ask a question. Even if you're not able to make a suggestion, your question may start the writer thinking.

Sample Writers' Group Session

Writer: The assignment is to describe a game in 75 words. My first draft is about 100 words. Here it is:
"Checkers is played on a board with 60 light and dark squares. Each player has 16 pieces. The object is to capture all the opponent's pieces by jumping over the pieces in a diagonal jump. At the start of the game, pieces can move only one square straight ahead, but if an opponent's piece is one square ahead, on a diagonal, you can jump it and capture it if there is an empty square on the other side. If your piece ends up on the last row, it is "kinged," meaning that it now has the ability to move anywhere on the board, but still one square at a time."

Listener 1: You covered a lot of facts in a few sentences.

Writer: Thanks. But I need to cut at least 25 words.

Listener 2: The board has 64 squares, not 60.

Writer: Ooops. You're right. I typed that by mistake.

Listener 1: Can you use a diagram? It could save some words.

Writer: That's a good idea.

Listener 2: Instead of "straight ahead," what if you wrote just "ahead"?

Listener 3: That might be less clear, though.

Writer: I'll think about it.

Listener 1: The phrase "by jumping over the pieces in a diagonal jump" seems wordy. Also, you use jump twice.

Writer: Mmmm. How about "by making diagonal jumps?"

Listener 2: Yes. That saves five words and it gets rid of the repetition.

Writer: Thanks for all the help. I think the next draft will be less wordy and clearer.

FREQUENTLY ASKED QUESTIONS

Copying: How can I help students avoid copying from encyclopedias and similar books when they write reports?
• Give them subjects that aren't in the books. For example, instead of a topic such as "Australia," try "The Similarities and Differences Between Australia and Canada."
• Give assignments that require format switching. For example, instead of an essay on Australia, students could write poems about Australia, or a travel brochure.
• Teach students to paraphrase. The secret is to take a few notes if needed, then put the original aside and describe the ideas in one's own words. The pitfall is trying to paraphrase while the original is in sight. (See page 23.)

Editing: How do I get students to improve their own work?
• Teach them editing skills using mock manuscripts. (See pages 12 and 28.)
• After they've finished an assignment, before collecting their work, give time in class for a "final edit." Focus their attention on specific issues, such as making sure the title is specific, making sure there are sufficient paragraph breaks, and eliminating run-on sentences. Don't overwhelm students with too many items. The goal is to create the editing habit.

Idea development: How do I teach students to develop an idea so that they go beyond the surface?
• Demonstrate the process on the board. Choose a topic, for example, "Cats make better pets than dogs," and show how *you* would think up arguments that support that idea. Then draft an essay on the board.
• Have students work together in small groups developing ideas. Their give-and-take parallels in visible form the development process that goes on inside a writer's mind.

Length: How can I wean students away from asking "How long does it have to be?" whenever I give an assignment.
• Don't! They're smart to ask the length of an assignment. Most writing is done to a set length. For example, newspaper columnists often turn out 800 words; movie writers produce scripts that average 110 pages. In other words, writing to "fit" is an important skill. For this reason, when giving an assignment, usually specify a rough length. Of course, an occasional "open ended" assignment can help students learn to discover how much is enough for a topic.

Motivation: How do I excite students about writing?
• Be a model for them. Write with them.
• Show interest in their work. This doesn't mean praise, which often is a shallow response. Instead, if you describe your true reactions ("I learned something new") and ask genuine questions, students will see that their work matters.
• Give assignments that make a difference. An example is having older students write skits that younger children perform. (See page 11 for more ideas.)
• Give assignments that relate to topics students really care about. What are these topics? Ask the students.
• Structure assignments so that students see for themselves that they have met the criteria. This means being specific about the task. For example, specify that a report include five facts that are new to everyone in the room. This challenge will push students to look for novel information. Or give an assignment that requires teaching someone (the teacher?) a new skill, such as eating with chopsticks or folding a paper airplane that will fly for at least five seconds. The proof of the writing will be in the doing.

Originality: How do I help students learn to write original stories instead of appropriating plots that they've encountered in movies and movies?
• Remember that Shakespeare and other great writers often based their writing on old tales. If students are drawn to a familiar story, suggest that they find a way to alter it, for example, by translating it into a new format or making the hero into the villain and the villain into the hero.
• Have students start from a person or character that interests them, for example, an uncle, a pet, or an old car. The next step is identifying something special about the subject, for example, the uncle's juggling ability. Then comes the crucial step, inventing a problem or challenge for the subject. The story will unfold as the character tries to solve the problem or meet the challenge. Will the character be successful? That question will keep the writer writing

Resources

■ ■

Plagiarism: How do I teach students not to do it?
• Explain that plagiarism is stealing, but the real victim is the plagiarizer who, by handing in someone else's work, misses an opportunity for developing important writing skills.
• Make absolutely clear the actions that you will take if you discover students plagiarizing.

Run-on sentences: How do I teach students not to run their ideas together in a tangle.
• Regularly write run-on sentences on the board and have students practice correcting the problem. It will help if you or students attempt to read aloud the run-on sentences.

Story Endings: How do I help students come up with satisfying story endings, not "And then I woke up"?
• Explain that a story's climax should relate to the main problem or conflict in the story. For example, if a character is trying to escape from a sinking ship, the ending will tell whether or not the character gets off the ship.
• Have students collect and classify different types of endings, for example, "return to the start" (*The Wizard of Oz*) or the unmasking ("Cinderella.") Then have students write stories using these forms.
• Have students give new endings to old stories.

Wording: How do I teach students to use precise language?
• Give students general words, and have them list words that are even more precise, for example: building-> house, cottage. Or: animal-> dog, collie, Lad (a particular collie).

How to Teach Writing Without Going Crazy © 1998 Monday Morning Books, Inc.